# Asset Protection Secrets

## Securing Family Wealth from Creditors, Predators and Politicians

# Asset Protection Secrets

## Securing Family Wealth from Creditors, Predators and Politicians

### By Ronald C. Morton, LL.M., AEP®, EPLS
#### Certified Elder Law Attorney®

Themis, LLC
2021

First Printing: 2021

ISBN 9798708620811

Themis, LLC
402 E. Main St.
Clinton, MS 39056

www.themislegal.us

# Dedication

To my loving family, Addison, Bailey,
and Cindy Morton


Thank you. Without your support and patience, I would
have never completed this work.

# Contents

# Acknowledgments

I would like to thank Kimberly Jenkins, Anna Coleman, Katie Anne Collins, Muriel Collins, and Kitty Kelsey for their assistance editing and proofreading the manuscript and for their helpful comments along the way.

# Preface

When picking up this book, you may be wondering why I have written it. The simple answer is to help prevent your family from losing everything in the event of your death. This book is about protecting you and your family. The average family in Mississippi knows very little about Estate Planning. They are unaware that without proper planning, their death could mean the financial destruction of their family's lives, or leave their family in a position of endless disputes in irreconcilable feelings of betrayal. Because of this, I have endeavored to get word out to the public so that no family has to watch their worldly possessions be taken away or squandered over needless bickering.

The purpose of this book is to inform you of the steps you can take to protect not only your assets but also the loved ones you leave behind. Though this type of planning protects your family when you pass, Estate Planning can also secure your belongings while you are still living. There are multiple threats to every estate and the title reflects this sad reality. Nobody should have to endure the loss of their childhood home after they have already suffered the loss of a loved one.

While writing this book, I found myself reflecting on the hundreds of families that my firm has already helped. Focusing on specific events that have come across my desk over the past two decades made me proud of the real impact that we have had and continue to have on the lives of Mississippi families. We have had the privilege to help guide families into planning that has protected them, their spouses and descendants from losing their homes, farms, and savings, and from paying significant and unnecessary income and estate taxes. This process gave me a real appreciation for our core purpose:

Protecting that which
our Clients Treasure most …
Everything they own,
and Everyone they Love

Through this book I want to provide you with this same valuable information we provide our clients, so you can keep your family and belongings secure and protected.

## Introduction

When considering protection of your assets, the term "estate planning" often conjures images of dry legalese, endless meetings with attorneys, and exotic tax planning for the super-rich. The reality for the overwhelming majority of people is that "estate planning" is simply the task of arranging your affairs so that the people you love are protected and provided for in the event of your death or disability. This type of future planning is easily and too often avoided because it requires us to recognize the uncomfortable certainty that one day each of us will die. Many do not plan as well as they could and fail to protect their assets due to a mistaken belief that estate planning, especially planning with trusts, is only necessary for the very wealthy. These people do not see planning as essential for them because their estate is "simple." They simply lack sufficient information to know all of their options so that their worldly possessions will pass to the people they want, in the way that they want, and at the time that they want, without unnecessary cost or delay. They believe the process is easy, perhaps even automatic, and that their assets are already in fairly good order. They assume the transfer of their assets will be smooth for their heirs when they pass, but they simply do not have sufficient understanding of the process to plan optimally.

It is unfortunate that so few appreciate the complete process because it is not just the wealthy that will benefit from proper planning. In fact, "regular people" with "simple estates" in many ways have the most to gain from planning because often the loss of any part of an inheritance will have a much greater impact on their families. It is a cruel and unfortunate irony that the wealthiest families who can most afford to lose assets frequently plan their estates to maximize asset preservation, while many families of much more modest means who will enjoy the greatest impact from inherited wealth are the most likely to lose assets due to lack of planning. For example, while a wealthy family with an estate of $20 million could lose up to $5 million of the family's assets due to death taxes because of poor planning, the family would still inherit $15 million after taxes were paid. While they would certainly rather not have been required to pay death taxes if they could avoid it, $15 million is still a substantial inheritance by any standard. But the family of much more modest means whose only asset is a small home and savings of $100,000 risks losing everything they have worked a lifetime for should their loved one enter a nursing home without a good plan in place. That family could wind up inheriting nothing if good planning were not done. To be fair, some estates are considerably larger and more complicated than others. Still, if you have a bank account, car, house, land, or anything else of value, either monetary or sentimental, you have an "estate." If you care anything about how your estate is passed down to your loved ones, you owe it to them to "plan" your estate prudently. This book will help.

Within this book, you will find the paths and options available to you when looking into planning your estate and protecting your assets. The process of planning your estate truly comes down to protecting all the people and possessions you hold most near and dear to your heart. Through the next few pages, I will educate you on many opportunities and benefits that a comprehensive estate plan will provide, not only in the management and distribution of your assets following your death but during your lifetime as well. This book is authored by a Mississippi Estate Planning Law Specialist, Accredited Estate Planner®, and Certified Elder Law Attorney® and is explicitly written for Mississippi residents. However, while providing you with a thorough summary of many estate planning techniques and opportunities, the book is no substitute for competent legal counsel. Many of the strategies discussed may appear to be simple or even intuitive because they are explained in easy-to-understand terms, but actual implementation can be quite complex. Most strategies discussed require professional help. In other words, this is not a "do it yourself" guide. The purpose of this text is to better prepare you to discuss your options and goals with your own estate planning attorney and other financial advisors. After reading the information provided, you will have a better understanding of how each element and planning opportunity fits into your overall plan.

For those readers that already have a plan in place, this book should serve to give a better understanding of how your estate actually operates, both during your lifetime and after death. It will likely explain some things already contained in your planning documents and give you a better understanding of why they are there and what they mean. It may even reveal some shortcomings of your existing plan and give you some additional planning tools to consider adding the next time you meet with your advisors. For readers without a plan, this book will give you an overview of many planning opportunities available to you, the relative benefits of each, and can serve as a basis for discussion with your advisors as you plan your estate.

## Why Plan Your Estate?

Recent surveys around the United States reveal that fewer than half of the adult population has done anything at all to protect their assets or plan their estates. If you happen to fall into that category, I have good news: The State of Mississippi already has done an estate plan for you! The estates of individuals who die without a Will are called "intestate" estates, and the state of Mississippi has implemented default rules for administering and dividing such estates. For more detailed information on probate of intestate estates, you may request a copy of The Probate Book at www.TheProbateBook.com.

First, these intestacy rules provide a list of relatives and other interested people that have priority to be appointed to administer the estate, known as the estate "administrator." The administrator is appointed by the Chancery Court in the county of residence of the person who died, also called the "decedent." The judge has broad discretion in appointing an administrator, but the law provides an order of preference in the selection. First in line to receive the title would be the surviving spouse. If there is no surviving spouse, then one of the children would be in the position to serve as an administrator. If there is no one willing to serve as administrator, each county has a "county administrator" appointed by the court to administer unrepresented estates, or the court can appoint someone else. One of the primary benefits of planning an estate is to remove this uncertainty of who will be appointed.

The process of administering an estate is called "probate." The purpose of probate is to allow creditors and other potential heirs to make any claims that they may have against the estate before the judge distributes the estate assets. Once all valid creditor claims have been satisfied and the judge determines the true heirs of the estate, intestate estates are ultimately divided equally between the spouse (if the decedent was married) and the children of the decedent. If there is no spouse, the assets are split equally among the children of the decedent, or if there are no children then to other close relatives. The descendants of deceased children will divide their parent's share.

If this default plan sounds like the way you want your estate handled, you may not need to read any further as the Mississippi intestacy law already has things satisfactorily planned for you, but most people want more say over how their affairs will be handled. For the individuals that want control over where and to whom their assets go when they pass, planning is necessary. The primary tools for planning an estate in Mississippi are Wills, Powers of Attorney, Revocable Living Trusts, Irrevocable Trusts, and in some limited circumstances, simply re-titling assets.

## The Goals of an Estate Plan

The goals and benefits of a good estate plan are best summarized as follows:

> **An estate plan allows you to distribute your assets to the people you want, in the manner you want, and at the time you want, while protecting them from government and creditor interference, delay, and confiscation.**

A comprehensive estate plan can accomplish all of this, even if you become incapacitated. These goals can be best achieved through four vehicles that will be discussed extensively in the chapters that follow.

**1. Will-** The most common vehicle to use when planning an estate is the Will. A validly executed Will takes effect upon your death, names the person that you choose to administer your estate, and distributes your estate precisely as instructed after your death. The distribution of your estate may be immediate and outright to your heirs or may involve some intentional delay for the recipient to gain some maturity or accomplish a specific goal before distribution. All of these can be controlled through the terms of your Will.

**2. Durable Power of Attorney-** The second primary document used in estate planning is a durable power of attorney or POA. Through the Power of Attorney, you can give to a third party of your choosing authority to act on your behalf in your absence, even if you become disabled. Your POA can be for a limited purpose only, such as permitting an individual to sell a house in your absence, or it may be general, granting your agent the authority to do anything that you could do yourself.

**3. Revocable Living Trust**- Another standard tool used by many in planning their estates is the Revocable Living Trust. While Revocable Living Trusts are not appropriate tools for every estate, they are frequently utilized for lifetime and post-death estate management. They are considered by most to be a more comprehensive planning alternative to a simple Will.

**4. Legacy Trust™**- A fourth and final tool used by many to protect their assets from probate, conservatorship, and loss to nursing home costs and Medicaid is the Legacy Trust™. The Legacy Trust™ is a flexible irrevocable trust that permits the creator to retain significant power to manage and even change many aspects of their estate plan and retain positive tax benefits over trust property but protect the trust assets from Medicaid in the event of a stay at a nursing home.

**5. Healthcare Documents** - Additional planning documents that should be included in every estate plan are the Power of Attorney for Healthcare, Health Insurance Portability and Accountability Act (HIPAA) Release, and an Advanced Healthcare Directives. These documents allow you, rather than a court, to name the people you want to make medical decisions for you if you are unable to do so yourself, and to have input into your care and treatment even during incapacity.

## Conclusion

In the chapters that follow, you will be presented with

summaries and explanations of the many estate planning opportunities available in Mississippi. None of these planning techniques are inherently right, wrong, best, or worst. They are each merely tools. Each method should be carefully considered in light of your overall goals, desires, budget, intended outcome, and the potential for unintended consequences arising from the management of your estate. In other words, you should use the correct tool to accomplish your goals. Just like every person and family is unique, every estate plan is tailor-made for the individual. There are no prefabricated plans that are right for every circumstance. There is no "one size fits all" solution. The goal of this book is to provide you with a thorough discussion of your planning options to assist you with determining the planning tools that are best for the management and distribution of your family's assets.

# Chapter 1: What is an Estate?

You don't have to be a Gates, Buffet, or Bezos to have an "estate." Your estate is comprised of all your assets. It is, in short, everything you own. Your assets can take many different forms – land, money, stocks, vehicles, jewelry, intellectual property, and personal belongings, just to name a few. The primary goal of planning an estate is usually the distribution of assets to your intended beneficiaries in the time and manner you desire. However, in planning your estate, you also should consider your intangible assets – the values, beliefs, and life-events that are important to you – which you desire to pass along to future generations. Comprehensive estate planning, or "Legacy Planning," can address passing down both your tangible and intangible assets to your loved ones.

## Personal Property

### Cash and Accounts

Cash and equivalent assets are generally held in bank or brokerage accounts. Occasionally real cash may be placed in a safe deposit box, personal home safe, gun safe, or even in the freezer. The most important aspect of dealing with cash assets, whether actual cash or account equivalents, is identifying the assets and the intended beneficiaries. Where cash or equivalent assets are held in accounts, transfers can occur through joint ownership or by naming a beneficiary. Such a beneficiary will be identified as a "Pay on Death" or "Transfer on Death" beneficiary, or with the letters POD or TOD followed by the intended recipient, in the account name. When planning your estate, you must be intentional and deliberate as to what you wish to accomplish through such title changes because it is usually the title of the asset, not the provisions of your Will, that controls distribution of jointly titled or TOD/POD assets.

**Example**: Jerry and Molly are in their second marriage, and each has children from a prior marriage. They have $100,000 in a jointly owned bank savings account. Jerry dies and provides in his will that his adult children, Jill, Sabrina, and Kelly, will each receive $10,000 from his savings account.

**The result:** Molly retains ownership of the entire $100,000. Because she was a co-owner of the account, the joint bank account assets did not pass through Jerry's estate since he was not the account owner at the time of his death. Jerry's intent that the money from his joint account be shared with his children was irrelevant. And unless Molly names Jerry's children in her planning documents, the money in that account will pass to Molly's children upon her death.

**Lesson:** Be careful and deliberate when titling assets and make sure that any specific bequests are directed from accounts that will be controlled by your estate following your death.

Discrepancies between account ownership and a Will can become especially problematic when a parent names one of multiple siblings as the co-owner of an asset or account. Such co-ownership is frequently made for the convenience of the parent, who, in many circumstances, is elderly and relies on the periodic assistance of her children. In other cases, the parent wishes to simplify asset transfer at death so that funds will be available for their funeral or so that assets can be accessed and distributed without probate. But in other circumstances, the parent intends for the surviving co-owner child to receive all the funds that remain in the account. A co-owner child will almost always be considered the owner of the account upon the parents' death, regardless of contrary provisions in their Will. The parent's Will does not control the distribution of a non-estate asset like a joint bank account. Likewise, the surviving co-owner child is the owner of the asset to the exclusion of the other children. In such an instance, the distribution to the other siblings would only be an unenforceable moral obligation and not legally compelled by the Will. Such unintended consequences almost always result in bitter feelings among those siblings who feel cheated out of their inheritance versus those of a caregiver sibling who is equally certain that the deceased parent's intent was to compensate him disproportionately because of that sibling's greater care and attention to their parent. You should take care to avoid such uncertainty when planning your estate.

Another issue that periodically arises concerning cash assets is whether a transfer of a cash container, i.e., the safe or freezer, is also a transfer of the cash contained in it.

**Example:** Dad had a safe deposit box containing $50,000 in cash. Dad had three children, Judy, Mary, and Sam, but only named his daughter Judy as a signatory to the box.

**The Result:** Upon Dad's death, uncertainty arises as to whether Judy is now the owner of the $50,000 or whether the $50,000 is part of Dad's estate to be shared with all three children. The outcome probably is that Judy owns all the cash in the box. However, there may be some basis to assert that the money should be shared.

**The Lesson:** While limited Mississippi law is available to assist in interpreting the result of this dispute, it would be far better for the parent to address the issue as part of her overall plan by making specific reference to the cash and stating her specific intent as to its use and distribution.

## Retirement Accounts

Retirement accounts are controlled by the terms of an agreement between the account owner and the account custodian. The terms of these contracts are primarily controlled by requirements of federal or state law and will vary depending on whether the plan is an ERISA plan, such as a 401(k), or a non-ERISA plan, such as an IRA. In either case, the ultimate distribution of those assets will be controlled by beneficiary designation, or in the case of ERISA plans where there is a surviving spouse, possibly by operation of Federal law. In either case, unless the estate is the named beneficiary or no beneficiary is named on the account at all, the transfer of these assets will occur outside of the estate. A provision inside of the Will designating someone other than the named beneficiary will be of no effect unless the named retirement account beneficiary is actually the estate. Otherwise, retirement assets pass according to the beneficiary designation and outside of the probate estate.

Because retirement accounts grow tax-deferred, there is a significant benefit to a continued deferral of these accounts for as long as possible. Individuals that inherit retirement assets have the option of withdrawing the funds immediately and paying tax on the entire withdrawal or withdrawing the funds in smaller increments over ten years. We call this latter option "stretching out" the distribution. In some limited circumstances such as a beneficiary spouse, minor child, or a disabled child, the stretch-out can be even longer than a decade, possibly even the life expectancy of the beneficiary. The advantage of this stretch is to delay payment of income taxes on the inherited funds until they are withdrawn. In addition to tax deferral, by stretching distributions from an inherited account, the recipient may be able to pay taxes on the funds at lower tax rates. While an individually named self-disciplined beneficiary can often affect this so-called "stretch out," the tax benefits are only stretched to the extent that the beneficiary does not prematurely withdraw the funds.

**Example 1**: Assume Son inherited an individual retirement account containing $100,000. Son's current highest income tax bracket is 20%, but Son will hit a 25% tax rate at $20,000 of additional income. If Son withdraws all $100,000 in the first year, he will pay $4,000 (20%) taxes on the first $20,000 withdrawn, and $20,000 taxes (25%) on the remaining $80,000. If Son had, instead, only withdrawn $20,000 per year for 5 years, Son would only pay total taxes of $20,000 – a savings of $4,000 – by only paying taxes at Son's current top tax bracket, and not moving into the next bracket.

Rather than leaving prudent withdrawal to chance, a parent can name a trust as the retirement beneficiary with instructions to delay distribution of the account assets in order to ensure optimized tax savings. An additional consideration may be whether a beneficiary has or is likely to have creditors. While retirement accounts in Mississippi are usually protected from creditor claims, an inherited retirement account likely does not share this protection. However, retirement accounts left in a properly drafted trust will protect inherited retirement funds from creditors. Both objectives can be accomplished through a Retirement Preservation Trust.

## Tangible Personal Property

Personal property is a general term used to describe all forms of property other than real estate. Different sections in this chapter deal with financial personal property, such as cash, stocks, bonds, bank accounts, brokerage accounts, and retirement accounts. However, in addition to these financial assets, everyone owns actual items of personal property, such as automobiles, furniture, equipment, jewelry, and other "stuff." These nonfinancial items of personal property are referred to as "tangible personal property." Just as it is essential to identify the recipients of financial assets, it is often imperative for estate plans to designate the intended beneficiary of tangible personal property. Sometimes this is because the personal property is very valuable, such as collectible artwork or precious metals. More frequently, however, identifying the recipients of tangible personal property upon the death of their owner is vital to avoid friction or hurt feelings in the family.

In many cases, the tangible personal property that an individual owns, while not inconsequential, usually does not comprise a substantial portion of the individual's estate value. In other words, from a purely monetary standpoint, most people's tangible personal property is simply not worth much. Yet, often these items of tangible personal property hold significant sentimental value to family members. Identifying the intended recipients of these pieces of tangible personal property will, at a minimum, ensure that family members recognize the intent of the deceased, even if they may ultimately disagree with the decision.

Alternatively, failing to identify the intended recipients of tangible personal property can result in feuds among family members, as one child raids the parent's home of cherished family heirlooms before the arrival of the other children. At best, this results in bruised feelings among surviving family members. At worst, the failure to identify the inheritor of these cherished heirlooms results in legal disputes between siblings over the ultimate distribution of this "stuff." A good estate plan will identify the intended recipients of specific tangible personal property if that is important to the owner and otherwise provide for an orderly process of dividing any remaining tangible personal property fairly among the surviving heirs.

**Real Estate**

Frequently individuals also own land or what is more formally referred to as real estate or real property. Real property, like personal property, can be bequeathed by its owner through a Will. As a practical matter, estates holding land almost always require probate because of the need to confirm a title change to the new heirs.

The purchaser of real property always requires

confirmation to the buyer's satisfaction that the sellers are the actual "owners" of the property. When property is acquired through purchase or gift, such confirmation is easily obtained through a review of the deeds on file in the courthouse. A deed transferring the property from its former owner to the new owners would be recorded, thereby giving the new purchaser satisfactory proof of its current ownership. However, where property is inherited, no such deed is on file. The decedent cannot sign a deed after death. Instead, the purchaser must satisfy himself or herself that the individuals purporting to be the new owners of the property are, in fact, the sole heirs. Additionally, the purchaser must also be satisfied that a deceased former owner did not die with unpaid indebtedness, because the decedent's outstanding creditors could have the ability to force the sale of the decedent's real property to cover those debts. The probate process addresses both concerns.

Through probate, the court will decide the decedent's heirs, thereby satisfying any later purchaser as to a complete and reliable list of the new owners of the real property. Likewise, the probate process identifies the claims of valid estate creditors. Accordingly, a purchaser could buy the property without concern that an unpaid creditor might force a sale of the property to satisfy the decedent's debts.

Where an owner bequeaths real property to an individual named in a Will, probate is also necessary to satisfy a purchaser of the legitimacy of the new ownership. The first act of a court in a probate action is to determine the validity of a decedent's Will, if one exists. Until a court has entered an order establishing a purported Will to be valid, the Will has no legal authority. Accordingly, an unprobated Will that bequeaths property to an individual is of no effect. A purchaser cannot rely on that Will until a court has entered an order declaring it to be valid. Such an order is obtained through probate.

As such, real property almost always requires probate, whether or not the owner died having executed a Will.

## Intangible Assets

Estate planning has traditionally focused on the tangible assets that an individual has accumulated over his lifetime. It almost always fails to address any intangible assets – those personal standards, values, and habits usually of the greatest import that have made you who you are and who you have become. These intangibles may take the form of family values, such as hard work and honesty, spiritual values, like faith and prayer, or family stories and opportunities that have changed your life. However, it is scarce indeed to find an estate plan that memorializes these intangibles. Traditional estate planning does little to capture the values, stories, or memories. In planning your Legacy, significant consideration should be given to incorporating your intangible assets into your overall plan. This may involve provisions in your Will expressing your statement of faith or values. It could include the creation of a separate document altogether, designed to capture your stories, events, memories, and values that you deem to be most important to you and ensure that they are passed along to future generations. While your family and loved ones will no doubt appreciate an organized plan for distributing your financial assets, a written expression of your formative events, stories, and core values will actually become a cherished family heirloom that will inform and remain meaningful to them and many future generations long after your estate is settled. There is no right or wrong way to incorporate this into your planning, but to ignore it altogether would be a lost opportunity indeed. There are numerous tools available to assist you in this endeavor, and it would be tragic to simply ignore passing along those aspects, which you have likely identified as being most important to you as part of your overall estate plan. For a free tool to capture and pass along your own intangible wealth to your family, visit www.BonaFideLegacy.com.

# Chapter 2: Your Will

As you have already seen in the introductory pages of this book, there are numerous advantages to planning your estate. The core document used in planning for the death of most individuals is their Last Will and Testament or simply their "Will." A Will is a document executed by you that expresses your intended wishes concerning the disbursement of your assets after your death. By writing and signing a Will, you take your estate out of Mississippi's default intestate statutes and substitute your plan for how you want your estate to be distributed.

## The Fundamentals of Will Creation

A Will is a solemn document with lasting legal consequences. As such, certain safeguards exist in Mississippi law to ensure that the Will is an expression of your desires, rather than the desires of someone else. These safeguards protect your estate from forgery, improper influence, or creation of a document that expresses something other than your intended desire for your estate's distribution at your death.

## Testamentary Capacity

For your Will to be valid, you must have the capacity to execute the Will. Capacity simply means that you understand (a) that you are signing a document governing the final distribution of your estate, (b) you understand who your children, spouse, and other close relatives are, and (c) you understand how your assets will be distributed.

Capacity also requires that you be at least eighteen years old to execute a valid Mississippi Will.

As you can see, this is not a very high standard. However, Wills executed in the absence of sufficient capacity, or where capacity is questionable, can result in a Will fight, or "contest." A Will contest is a lawsuit usually filed as part of the estate proceedings, where someone challenges the validity of the Will document submitted to the court because the deceased person lacked the required minimum legal capacity or was under the influence of another when it was signed. This type of lawsuit is costly, both in real dollars and in the emotional toll to your surviving heirs. Accordingly, prudence dictates that every effort be made to show proper capacity at the time of the Will's signing to minimize the likelihood of unnecessary and protracted Will-contest litigation.

**Witnesses**

For a Will to be valid in Mississippi, two credible individuals must witness it. The witnesses are attesting to your competence, and your expression that the document you are signing is intended to serve as instructions for the distribution of your assets following your death. While there is no requirement that your signature, or the signatures of the witnesses, actually be notarized, it is a wise practice to have all signatures notarized so that an affidavit can later be submitted to a court as sworn testimony to the validity of your and their signatures. The notarized witness affidavits serve as a substitute for the testimony of the witnesses when the Will is ultimately presented to the court for probate instead of their live testimony.

## Beneficiaries

One of the primary advantages of executing a will, rather than relying upon the intestacy statutes of Mississippi, is your ability to name the beneficiaries of your estate. These beneficiaries may or may not be your natural heirs. Capacity only requires that you know who your children are, not that you leave them anything. In fact, the only ways to distribute your estate to people other than your natural beneficiaries upon your death is to transfer title of the assets to them or a trust for their benefit during your lifetime, name them as co-owners during your lifetime, name them as POD/TOD beneficiaries on the account, or through the execution of a Will.

## Estate Executor

If you die with a valid will, your estate will be administered by the person you appoint. We call this person the "executor" or "executrix." An executor is, in many ways, like the administrator of an intestate estate, but with two crucial differences. First, while the appointment of an administrator is left to the sole discretion of a chancery judge, you get to decide who will be the executor of your estate. In other words, if you execute a will, you get to decide who manages your estate instead of a court making that decision for you. Second, by drafting a will, you have the right to waive the requirement that the executor post a bond. While posting a bond may be advisable in some circumstances, if you feel the person you have named as executor is competent and honest, the purchase of a bond becomes an unnecessary and sometimes burdensome expense to the estate, costing the estate money that you would probably rather see distributed to your heirs. While courts have the discretion to waive this, not all do so in the absence of a Will waiving it. You can also expand the powers that your executor has in settling and managing your estate beyond what the law provides.

## Spousal Rights

Most married individuals name their spouse as the sole primary beneficiary of their estate. In this manner, the Will alters the default intestacy provisions, which only give the surviving spouse an equal child's portion of the estate. Occasionally, a decedent wants to limit, reduce, or even eliminate their spouse's right to inherit from her. In these circumstances, Mississippi law provides certain protections to ensure that the widowed spouse is not left impoverished. Specifically, Mississippi law gives every surviving spouse the right to elect against the will, meaning that the spouse has the right to claim a child's share of the estate if the surviving spouse is otherwise left with a smaller portion of the estate than a child's share. If such an election is made and the spouse's separate assets exceed 20% of the value of the child's share, then the child's portion payable to the spouse is reduced by the value of spouse's separate assets. In other words, although a will can alter the default estate plan in favor of a surviving spouse, the will cannot generally result in the surviving spouse receiving less than they would have otherwise received if the decedent had died without a will.

For individuals wishing to leave their surviving spouse with a smaller portion of their estate, the parties should enter into an agreement waiving this right of spousal election altogether. This is frequently done in cases of second marriages where one or both of the spouses have children from a prior marriage. Such a marital agreement can ensure that each party's respective heirs receive their full share of inheritance as if the second marriage had never occurred. An agreement should not be hastily entered into, and both parties should receive the benefit of separate counsel before consenting to such a marital agreement.

## The Right of Children to Inherit

Unlike spouses, children do not have a right to inherit anything under a Will in Mississippi. Under law it is perfectly acceptable to disinherit your child completely. Though this seems harsh, there are many reasons that parents disinherit their children or leave them with less than an equal share with their siblings. Such reasons include behavior which, in the parent's view, would result in the child's share of the estate being squandered, cruel or inappropriate treatment to the parent, a belief that the child has less need for a full portion of the inheritance than their siblings because of their independent success, or sometimes because a child is receiving public benefits that the parent fears would be lost if the child received their inheritance. In the case of this last circumstance, there are superior planning options to the disinheritance of a child that should be considered. For a discussion of planning opportunities available for disabled or special needs children, please see

Chapter 9.

## Specific Bequests and the Residuary

Generally, the distributions made from a Will fall within two types of bequests – specific and residuary. A specific bequest refers to a particular asset being transferred to specifically identified individuals or groups of individuals. Specific bequests frequently take the form of lists of items to be transferred to individual children, grandchildren, or siblings. The other dispositive provisions of a will usually involve everything that is left after creditors are paid, and specific bequests are made. This leftover portion is called the residue of the estate.

# Chapter 3: Probate

"Probate" is the court-supervised process of transferring the property formerly owned by deceased people to living people. Some property can be passed to co-owners or specifically identified beneficiaries without going through probate. Many of these probate-substitutes are discussed in Chapter 4. The rest must generally be accounted for through a formal court-supervised probate process before it can be legally distributed to surviving heirs or beneficiaries. This legal process is called "estate administration" or "probate." Probate occurs regardless of whether the deceased individual dies with or without a valid Will. While a will can streamline the probate process, it seldom eliminates it. The probate process is similar whether the individual died with a Will or died intestate. Both processes are described generally in this chapter. For more detailed information on the probate process, order *The Probate Book* at www.theprobatebook.com. Unfortunately, many people mistakenly believe that the execution of a valid Will avoids probate. This is simply not the case.

## Why Do We Have to Probate?

The probate process exists for three simple reasons. First, when a person dies, there is no longer a reliably identifiable owner of their property. It is crucial then, after a person's death, to have an orderly process of determining the new owners of the property. A second reason for probate is to protect creditors who are entitled to be re-paid from the deceased person's assets before they are distributed to the new owners. The probate case gives creditors a forum and opportunity to assert their claim. We call the act of submitting a claim for repayment from a deceased person's property "probating" a claim. A third reason for the probate process is protection of the record of property ownership so that individuals purchasing inherited property can, with confidence, know they are dealing with the lawful owners of the property and are acquiring a legal title. Without a reliable record of title, people would be reluctant to buy land or other assets formerly belonging to a deceased individual out of fear of an unknown creditor claim or an unknown heir that might have superior rights to the property.

Each of these reasons exists, regardless of whether the deceased individual had a Will at the time of their death or died without one. Accordingly, the probate process applies to both types of estates. We call the estates of people who died after having signed a valid Will a "testate" estate. Conversely, when an individual dies without the benefit of a valid Will, we call the estate "intestate."

### Opening the Estate

The probate process begins with the filing of a petition to open the estate, usually in the county of the decedent's place of residence. Where the decedent had a Will, the person entitled to open the estate and serve as the decedent's representative is generally named in the Will. In the absence of a Will, or in cases where those named in the Will are unable or unwilling to serve, any interested person may file the petition to open the estate. However, state law gives an order of preference, beginning with spouses and children.

In estates where a valid Will has been executed, the person charged with oversight of the estate is called the estate's "Executor" if male or "Executrix" if female. Similarly, in the absence of a Will, the appointed estate manager is called the "Administrator" if male or "Administratrix" if female. For ease of use, the masculine form of each will be used through the remainder of this book when referencing the estate's personal representative. The petition that opens the estate will tell the Court and the public at large whether the individual died with a valid Will, where the individual resided at the time of death, and the reasons that the Court is being asked to appoint the proposed individual to the role of Administrator or Executor. Where the deceased individual had a valid Will, a copy and the original are also provided to the Court for determination of its validity. If the Will appears to be valid, the original is then filed in the official records of the Chancery Court, and the copy is filed with the court records and available for public viewing.

Before admitting a Will for probate, the court must first be presented with sufficient evidence that the Will is, in fact, valid. In most cases, this is accomplished through the testimony of at least one witness who was present when the decedent signed the Will. Usually, that testimony is presented to the court through an affidavit. An affidavit is simply a sworn statement of facts that is attested to by an individual under oath and penalty of perjury. That is why lawyers will frequently have witnesses sign an affidavit at the same time they sign the Will. This affidavit can later serve as their "testimony" when the Will is submitted for probate instead of live testimony. The court will also review the original Will for any suspicious irregularities and sufficient evidence of testamentary intent before pronouncing it to be valid. The court will specifically look for language in the Will that confirms that the document is an expression of the signing party's intent to make a final distribution of their assets following their death. Generally, no notice to creditors, beneficiaries, or heirs is required to admit a Will into probate or to open the estate of a person who died without a Will.

### Does Probate Require the Services of a Lawyer?

Every estate, regardless of whether opened with or without a Will, requires the services of a licensed attorney. The reason for this is twofold. First, as a practical matter, the probate process is highly technical, and courts rely upon the skill and expertise of attorneys to ensure that the technical requirements of the law are complied with before distributing assets to beneficiaries. Additionally, once an estate is opened, the estate becomes a separate and distinct legal entity, in the same way, that corporations, trusts, and limited liability companies are separate legal entities. Unlike individuals, legal entities cannot act on their own. They must act instead through individuals. While individuals have the legal right to represent themselves before courts, legal entities enjoy no such ability. Accordingly, they must be represented by individuals or firms who are licensed by the state to act on behalf of others, i.e., lawyers. Since the individuals named to carry out the wishes of a deceased individual, either as the Administrator or Executor, are not acting in their individual capacity, they have no standing to represent the legal entity (the estate) before the court in the absence of a license to practice law. So, the Executor or Administrator must hire a lawyer to represent the estate before the court. This is why, in every estate other than those where the named Administrator or Executor is a licensed attorney, an attorney must be hired to represent the estate. In recognition of this, Mississippi Uniform Chancery Court Rule 6.01 requires that a licensed attorney represent every estate.

## Is the Estate Required to Use the Same Attorney that Drafted the Will?

While an attorney must represent every estate, there is no requirement that the estate hire the lawyer who drafted the will. While some lawyers will go so far as to recommend themselves or even name themselves as the attorney for the estate in the Will, this practice is viewed by many to be unethical. It is not binding on the estate's representative. The Executor is free to hire whomever they choose. Of course, while not compelled to use their services, it is also not uncommon for the Executor to engage the services of the drafting lawyer to represent the estate. The drafting lawyer would already be familiar with the estate plan, the decedent's assets, the decedent, and often the decedent's family, and as such, is frequently the best choice to represent the estate.

## Determination of Heirs

One final and vital distinction between testate and intestate estates involves heirs. A well-drafted Will should identify the intended beneficiaries of a decedent, as well as the natural heirs of the decedent, especially when the heirs and beneficiaries are not the same. In the absence of a Will naming the natural heirs and intended beneficiaries, it usually becomes necessary to file an action to determine heirship to assure that all heirs have been identified and had an opportunity to appear before estate assets are distributed.

In a testate estate, the Will determines the distribution of the estate, regardless of the identity or existence of other natural beneficiaries (other than a spouse). Accordingly, an action to determine heirship is usually unnecessary intestate estates (although some judges still require it). The absence of this separate procedure can save the estate thousands of dollars in unnecessary expense and months of undue delay.

## Duties of Executors and Administrators

Other than the Executor's obligation to follow specific instructions in the Will, the role, duties, obligations, and actions of Executors and Administrators are identical. Both must act faithfully using the vigilance, diligence, and prudence of a person of discretion and intelligence managing their affairs. The Executor and Administrator must step into the shoes of the decedent to identify and safeguard the decedent's property. They must do this for the benefit of the decedent's creditors and then ultimately for the benefit of the heirs and beneficiaries. Inherent in this duty is the obligation to identify and secure the decedent's assets, to locate the decedent's creditors, and to locate and identify heirs and beneficiaries. Administrators and Executors are prohibited from personally benefiting from any estate assets in the absence of specific language in the

Will to the contrary.

This means that they may not borrow or personally use any of the estate assets and may not directly or indirectly purchase or acquire any interest in estate assets in the absence of provisions in the Will permitting them to do so. They also may not remove estate property from Mississippi. Further, the Executor may not loan any estate assets to a close relative or the estate's attorney. Administrators and Executors must act in a "fiduciary" capacity, meaning that they owe a duty of loyalty and good faith to the beneficiaries and creditors of the estate. They must act in the best interest of someone other than themselves.

## Temporary Administrator

On some occasions, it is necessary to delay the appointment of a permanent Administrator. In those circumstances, the court may appoint a temporary Administrator to perform the functions of estate administration while the regular administrator of the estate is being determined. This appointment may be made at the request of a creditor or any other interested person. The temporary Administrator has whatever duties and powers that the court has deemed appropriate and can be authorized to take charge of, preserve, and administer the estate during their term of appointment. The Temporary Administrator's term of engagement ends once a regular Administrator or Executor is appointed.

## Letters of Administration and Letters Testamentary

Once a court enters an order appointing an Administrator or Executor, the named individual must take an oath before the court clerk and post any required bond.

After that, the clerk will issue Letters of Administration in intestate estates or Letters Testamentary intestate estates. These "Letters" are legal documents containing the clerk's seal certifying that an individual has the legal authority to act on behalf of the estate. The issuance of fiduciary letters by the clerk of court gives others the proof of the appointed fiduciary's authority to act on behalf of the decedent and the decedent's estate. These Letters are the fiduciary's "keys" to accessing what would otherwise be the inaccessible private information of the decedent. Information concerning the decedent's banking and finance records, medical records, insurance policies, retirement accounts, and other information protected by privacy laws or traditionally treated as confidential becomes immediately accessible to the fiduciary once the clerk issues letters.

## Oath and Bond

A prerequisite to the issuance of Letters of Administration and Letters Testamentary is the taking of the oath by the appointed estate fiduciary and posting of an appropriate bond unless the court waives the requirement. The oaths for both Administrators and Executors are similar. Both must swear that they will honestly and competently discharge their duties as required by law. In addition, the Executor must swear that the Will submitted to the court is the most recent one. Similarly, the Administrator must attest to the best of their knowledge that there is no Will.

A sufficient bond is required of both Executors and Administrators unless the requirement has been waived.

Executors can be relieved of the requirement for posting bond if a waiver is contained in the Will. An Administrator must post bond in an amount equal to the value of the decedent's personal property; however, bond may be waived or reduced in the chancellor's discretion.

Anytime a court determines that the required bond is insufficient, an additional bond may be required. Where heirs have minimal concerns over an Administrator's handling of an estate, it is generally in their interest to request a waiver since the cost of bond is an expense of estate administration that will ultimately be paid or reimbursed from the assets of the estate. If all heirs of an estate do not join in the request to eliminate or reduce bond, or in the absence of language in a will authorizing waiver, bond must be set in an amount equal to the full value of the estate.

**Inventory**

One of the most fundamental roles of every estate fiduciary is the determination of the decedent's assets and protection of those assets for the benefit of the decedent's creditors and beneficiaries. The decedent's personal property must be used to satisfy any creditor claims before the estate may use the decedent's real property to fulfill those obligations. This is true in every intestate estate, and in the absence of a contrary provision in a decedent's will, it is equally applicable intestate estates. Personal property remaining after all valid estate claims and expenses have been paid will then be distributed by the estate fiduciary to surviving heirs and beneficiaries. Without contrary instructions contained in a Will, an estate fiduciary must seek permission from the court to sell a decedent's real property to satisfy the valid obligations of the estate.

Accordingly, a fundamental and immediate role of both Administrators and Executors is to locate and account for all of the decedent's personal property. They are required to file a list of all assets and debts with the court within 90 days of being appointed. This list is called an "inventory." The inventory must be supplemented as often as necessary as new assets and debts are discovered. Additionally, Executors and Administrators are required to file inventories with the court annually. Courts often will waive the requirement for an inventory where the Will requests this.

## Exempt Property

Not all of a decedent's property is available to pay claims and expenses of the estate. Certain property is exempt from creditors under Mississippi law. The Administrator or Executor must set aside exempt property for the benefit of the decedent's surviving spouse and children. The exempt assets of an estate are: mechanic's tools; clothing; up to $10,000 of tangible personal property; up to $50,000 of life insurance payable to the estate, and equity of up to $75,000 in the decedent's residence inherited by children or grandchildren. This exempt property is unavailable for payment of creditor claims, administrative expenses, or even expenses of last illness and funeral. The exempt property is simply excluded from the estate and is instead distributed directly to the surviving spouse or descendants.

## One Year's Support

A surviving spouse and children who are receiving support from the decedent at his time of death are also entitled to one year's support from the assets of the decedent's estate as a priority claim. If a surviving spouse is separated from the decedent at the time of death, the surviving spouse must show that the separation was not his own choice or fault. The Executor or Administrator must determine the amount necessary to provide a year's support, although this determination is ultimately subject to the court's approval. The allowable support is the sum of money needed to purchase the necessary clothing for the spouse and children, to pay tuition for the children, and to otherwise provide for the comfortable support of the spouse and children for one year. This one-year support is of the highest priority and must be paid whether or not the estate is solvent. The request from a supported spouse or child for a year's support may be filed any time before the estate is closed. The final calculation of the year's support lies with the chancellor. The court is instructed to consider as part of its analysis the value of the estate, the rights of other estate beneficiaries, and the standard of living in which the decedent's dependents had become accustomed.

## Notice to Creditors

As stated earlier, one of the primary reasons to administer an estate is to provide an orderly method of determining and paying creditor claims. Accordingly, one of the essential functions of an Administrator or Executor after locating and securing a decedent's personal property is to locate and determine the people and entities to which the decedent owed money. This is accomplished through the mailed notice to known creditors and the publication of a notice to unknown creditors. Once creditors have been given notice that an estate has been opened, they must file a claim for any amount they are owed with the court within 90 days of the first publication of the formal notice. The Executor or Administrator must make reasonably diligent efforts to identify those persons and entities that have claims against the estate. The notice to known or suspected creditors must be mailed to their last known address. Once all known and suspected creditors have been notified and after a reasonably diligent search by the estate fiduciary, the estate fiduciary must file an affidavit with the clerk of court swearing to her reasonably diligent efforts in identifying potential creditors and specifically identifying those persons and entities to which notice was mailed. Upon mailing a written notice to all known claimants and filing an affidavit acknowledging such by the estate fiduciary with the court, notice to unknown creditors can then be published in a newspaper circulated in the county where the estate is pending. The notice must be published for three consecutive weeks, and the proof of that publication must be filed with the court clerk.

## Medicaid Recovery

Federal law requires states to seek recovery of Medicaid dollars spent on the decedent for skilled nursing care services and related home services. This is commonly known as "Medicaid Estate Recovery." Accordingly, the Mississippi Division of Medicaid must be noticed as a known creditor of every deceased Medicaid recipient. In every case in which the Medicaid recipient was 55 years of age or older when receiving Medicaid assistance, the Mississippi Division of Medicaid may seek recovery of payments made for nursing facility services, home and community-based services, and related hospital and prescription drug services from the recipient's estate. However, Medicaid's claim will be waived where the Medicaid recipient is survived by a spouse, a minor or dependent child, or a dependent blind or disabled child of any age. Exempt property that passes outside of a decedent's estate is not subject to the claims of creditors, including any claim for reimbursement filed by the Mississippi Division of Medicaid.

## Probate of Claims

For an Executor or Administrator to pay a claim against an estate, the claim must first be properly documented with the clerk of court. The process of a creditor filing documentation of their claim is commonly called "probating" the claim. This open process of presentment of claims in a public forum allows the Executor, Administrator, or any other interested person to contest claims which they believe are invalid. The requirement for creditors to make their claims public gives all interested people notice of the claims made and the ability to challenge the validity of any claim, or to hold the estate fiduciary personally responsible for payment of an invalid claim. The public nature of the process also prevents the Administrator or Executor from secretly paying claims favoring some claimants over others. To probate a claim, a claimant must present written evidence of the claim to the clerk of court within 90 days of the date of the first publication of notice to creditors. Claims based on written instruments such as promissory notes must include a copy of the original note or instrument. If the basis of the claim is a judgment or decree, the claimant must include a certified copy of the pleading. Where there is no written evidence of the claim, the claimant must present a signed itemized statement of the claim to the clerk in support of the claim. Every claim must be accompanied by an affidavit executed by the claimant. The clerk of court then admits conforming claims to probate. While the court must ultimately accept the claim for it to be paid, the failure of a creditor to timely file a claim will bar payment of that claim regardless of its validity.

Creditors holding security interests in a decedent's property like a home mortgage or lien on a car are not required to probate their claim. They can instead enforce their security interest, notwithstanding a complete failure to probate a claim. However, where a creditor's foreclosure or execution on their security interest results in a deficiency judgment, the secured creditor who fails to timely probate a claim is barred from collecting any deficiency from estate assets.

**Payment of Claims**

Administrators and Executors should speedily pay all claims due to an estate. However, they cannot pay any claims where the estate has insufficient assets to pay all claims. Likewise, they may not pay any claim that has not been first validly probated with the court. Any time a claim's validity is questioned by the Administrator or Executor, it should not be paid until a judicial determination of its efficacy is obtained. Accordingly, to be safe, claims are frequently not paid until immediately before the estate is closed, and a court order can be obtained, permitting each claim payment.

**Contesting Claims**

The Executor or Administrator, together with any heir or other creditor, may contest the validity of any probated claim. This right of third parties to contest claims is one of the reasons that the claims are required to be made public. Once challenged, the burden of establishing the validity of the claim rests with the creditor. No presumption of the claim's validity arises from the fact that it was timely filed.

**Sale of Personal Property**

Personal property of the estate can be sold to pay the debts of the estate or when it is otherwise in the best interest of all parties concerned. Where the cash and other liquid assets of an estate are insufficient to pay the validly probated claims and other valid debts and obligations of the estate, the Administrator or Executor must liquidate the personal property of the estate to meet these estate obligations. Although an Executor or Administrator may

31

sell any personal property of the decedent without a court order if the purpose of the sale is to pay debts of the estate, details of the sale must still be reported to the court. Usually, they will get court authority before selling any personal property. In addition, creditors can compel the sale of personal property for the payment of their claims.

### Sale of Real Property

Before any heirs can get marketable title to the real property of an estate, the creditor's claims must all be satisfied. Where there is insufficient cash and personal property in the estate to satisfy creditors, a court can permit the sale of land to repay debts. Additionally, where a decedent leaves a Will granting authority or direction to the Executor to sell real property, a court order authorizing the sale is not even necessary.

In the absence of authority to sell real property in a decedent's Will, no one can do so without a court order. There are only three circumstances in which a court can authorize the sale of real property from an estate:

1. **Prior Contract** - When a decedent enters into a contract to sell real property and does not complete the sale before the time of his death.
2. **Personal Property Insufficient to Pay Debts** - When the personal property is insufficient to pay the estate's debts and expenses, the court may order the sale of enough land to pay the debts and expenses of the estate.

3. **"To the Interest of" Heirs and Beneficiaries** - Where the sale of land is in the interest of the heirs and beneficiaries of an estate, the law permits the court to order the sale of land.

Before a court can order the sale of land, all interested parties must be given notice of the potential sale and will have the opportunity to oppose the sale. Additionally, every heir or other interested person has the absolute right to prevent the sale if that person posts bond payable to the Executor or Administrator in an amount fixed by the court which is sufficient to pay the debts and expenses of the estate not otherwise covered by the estate's personal property.

Once a court has ordered the sale of real property, the Executor or Administrator must post a bond in an amount equal to the sale price before the sale unless the court waives the requirement for bond. The court has the discretion to waive the bond if the sale is to occur after the 90-day creditor deadline has expired, and all of the beneficiaries have joined in the waiver request. Instead of bond, the chancellor may require the sale proceeds to be held in trust by the Executor, Administrator, or some other qualified person, such as the estate's lawyer, until such time that the court orders the release of the sale proceeds.

## Insolvent Estates

When the assets of a decedent are not sufficient to pay the debts and costs of administration of the estate, the estate is "insolvent." No inheritance will pass to the heirs of an insolvent estate other than exempt property and priority claims. Instead, the claims will be paid in the following priority:

*First Priority*: Exempt property will be distributed directly to the estate beneficiaries. Additionally, any provision for one year of support to a surviving spouse and children will be paid.

*Second Priority*: Cost and expenses of the decedent's last illness, funeral, and estate administration, including the executor or administrator's fee and the attorney's fee will be paid.

*Third Priority*: Any remaining funds will be distributed pro-rata to remaining creditors.

## Determination of Heirs

When someone dies without a will, Mississippi law determines who inherits the estate assets. This is accomplished through a court hearing called an heirship hearing, which is publicly advertised to give notice to all potential heirs of their opportunity to be declared an heir entitled to inheritance. Likewise, when a person's will fails to identify their heirs, an heirship hearing also becomes necessary.

## Who Inherits the Estate

After all costs of estate administration and creditor claims have been paid, the remaining assets of an estate are distributed to the heirs or beneficiaries. When an individual dies with a will, the will usually identifies the individuals or entities that will inherit. Often this is done through specific bequests, where individuals are identified to receive specific pieces of personal and real property. Additionally, most wills have a catch-all clause, called a "residuary." This term refers to everything that is left over – the residue once all specific bequests have been distributed. In the absence of specifically identified individuals or a class of individuals designated to receive the residuary of the estate, all estate assets remaining will be distributed according to the Mississippi law governing dissent and distribution of estate assets. Similarly, intestate estates are also distributed according to the law of dissent and distribution.

The law of descent and distribution transfers a decedent's estate among surviving relatives within certain classes of relationship to the decedent. The first group consists of the deceased individual's children and the descendants of any children who predeceased the decedent, along with the decedent's surviving spouse and any adopted children. If a decedent has any individuals in this first group, his estate will be distributed in equal shares to their children and spouse. If there are any predeceased children with descendants of their own, i.e., grandchildren of the decedent, then those descendants will share equally among the portion that would otherwise have been distributed to their deceased parent. In other words, grandchildren will receive their parents' share by representation if their parent is deceased.

If the decedent does not have any surviving relatives in this first group, his assets will be distributed among his parents, siblings, or survivors of any deceased siblings, i.e., nieces and nephews, in equal shares by representation. In the absence of any surviving relatives in this second class, the decedent's estate will be distributed among grandparents, aunts, and uncles in equal shares, but without rights of representation to cousins. In the rare instance that a decedent does not have any relatives within this class, the law will distribute the decedent's estate to the decedent's nearest blood relatives of the highest degree. Finally, where an individual dies without any blood relatives, their property will escheat to the State of Mississippi, as the inheritor of last resort. While this is possible, it is very rare. As you can see, the persistent rumor that "If you don't have a will, the State of Mississippi inherits all of your property" is simply not true, except in the rarest of circumstances.

### Closing the Estate

Whenever an estate has been administered by payment of debts and collection of assets, the Executor or Administrator must file a final accounting unless the court has waived such requirement. The accounting shows the court all the balances, income, charges, and disbursements while the estate has been opened supported by documentation. All heirs will be given notice and opportunity to appear at the presentation of the final accounting to the court; however, most heirs waive their right to attend. Once the accounting has been approved, the court will enter an order authorizing the executor or administrator to distribute the estate assets pursuant to the proposed plan and, upon completion of the distribution, will discharge them of any further duties and close the estate.

### Executor's and Administrator's Fees

Executors and Administrators are entitled to a reasonable fee for their services, along with reimbursement from the estate for all costs and expenses associated with administering the estate. In determining the amount of the Administrator's or Executor's fee to be awarded, the court must consider the amount of work the Executor or Administrator performed in making out reports, collecting and distributing assets, the skill required for the work undertaken, the responsibility involved, the amounts of money involved, and the promptness and efficiency with which the estate was administered and brought to a close. Where the estate has not been properly administered, the court may deny some or the entire Executor's or Administrator's fee.

## Attorney's Fees

Every Executor or Administrator must retain an attorney to represent him in administering an estate. The attorney's fees are the responsibility of the Executor or Administrator. However, these fees can be reimbursed from the estate upon authorization from the court as long as they are reasonable and benefit the estate. In awarding attorney's fees, courts will consider several factors including the skill required; the responsibility undertaken; the monetary value of the estate administered; liquidity; the speedy disposition of the business; the services of the attorney; the fees charged by other lawyers for similar services; the complexity of the issues; and the necessity of litigation. The most useful starting point for determining the amount of a reasonable fee is usually the number of hours reasonably expended on the estate, multiplied by the lawyer's reasonable hourly rate.

## Will My Estate Owe Estate Taxes?

A federal estate tax is imposed for every decedent's estate, whose net value exceeds $11,700,000 (in 2021). This amount is adjusted annually by the IRS for inflation, although it is currently set to drop to $5.85 million (indexed for inflation) in 2026. This amount can effectively be doubled for married couples where all the assets are left to the surviving spouse if an estate tax return is filed within nine months following the death of the first spouse. The first spouse's exemption is "ported" over to the surviving spouse, thereby giving the surviving spouse a double exemption. A similar result can also be accomplished by the creation of a trust by the first spouse to die, which utilizes the deceased spouse's estate tax exemption. The federal estate tax return is due nine months after a decedent's death, though it can be extended for an additional six months. Mississippi has imposed an estate tax upon a decedent's net estate equal to the maximum amount of the state death tax credit permissible in computing the federal estate tax payable by the estate. Currently, Mississippi does not have a separate inheritance tax.

# Chapter 4: Substitutes for Wills and Trusts

As the previous chapter makes clear, the probate process can be frustrating, time-consuming, and expensive. Understandably, many people want to avoid it where possible. Most people are not satisfied with the default plan for the distribution of their assets created by the state. However, in order to obtain a different result for distribution of assets, planning must be done. The most common form of planning for distributions of estate assets is through Wills and Trusts, but some try to avoid these planning options. They believe that doing their planning through a Will or Trust will be too expensive, time-consuming, or simply think that their estate is too basic to require such complex planning. Options do exist for individuals that want a different result from the default plan but are unwilling to draft wills or trusts. This chapter examines several of these substitute planning methods.

## Outright Transfer

One obvious opportunity to avoid the probate process is through a lifetime gifts. The outright transfer of property in this manner is quick, easy, often involves little or no legal assistance, and ensures ownership to the intended party. These types of transfers that are made during the grantor's lifetime are called "*inter vivos*" transfers. However, there are many drawbacks to using lifetime gifts as a substitute for estate planning.

The first major drawback to this form of planning is its permanence. You can change your will, beneficiary designations, and most trusts before you die, but once you give property away, it legally belongs to the recipient, and they have the authority to do anything they want with it thereafter, whether you approve or not. This may include selling property that you intended to remain in the family for future generations, or perhaps giving the property away to someone else. Sometimes the gifted property is lost to creditors of the gift recipient as a result of a lawsuit. Other times the gifted property passes outside the family because of divorce or a death in the family. With the outright transfer of property, the grantor loses all control over the property and has no right to undo the gift. Sometimes a grantor's health changes after they have given property away, and they need the property to pay for their care. However, unless the gift recipient is willing and able to give the property back, the grantor has no legal recourse to force the return of the property. This can even result in the denial of much needed Medicaid benefits to the grantor should they enter a skilled nursing facility within five years of making the gift.

**Example**: Mary is 80 years old and owns a home worth $280,000 and $100,000 in cash that she does not want to lose if she enters a nursing home. Mary gives her home and all of her money to her daughter, Tina. Two years later, Tina is charged and convicted of embezzling $500,000 from her employer and sentenced to five years' imprisonment and required to pay restitution.

**The Result**: Tina loses all of her assets, including the home and all the cash that Mary transferred to her.

**The Lesson**: Assets transferred to a child are subject to the risk of loss as a result of the child's creditors, bad judgment, mistakes, or just bad luck.

Another potential negative consequence of lifetime transfers is the federal gift tax and the loss of a stepped-up basis. All transfers made during an individual's lifetime over the annual exclusion, which is currently $15,000, must be reported on a gift tax return. If collective lifetime gifts exceed the lifetime gift exclusion, they are subject to tax. While most people never reach their lifetime gift limit of $11.7 million (in 2021), they nevertheless must file a gift tax return to report annual gifts that exceed $15,000 to any recipient.

A far more significant issue for most people, is the increase of future income taxes due to the loss of a "stepped up" basis. Income taxes are owed on the difference between the price paid for property, and its later sale price.

**Example**: Mary is 80 years old and owns a home worth $280,000 that she does not want her daughter to lose if she enters a nursing home. Mary purchased the home 40 years ago for $80,000. Mary gives her home to her daughter, Tina. Two years later, Mary dies, and then Tina sells the house.

**The Result**: Mary immediately loses her homestead exemption on the home. Additionally, Tina must pay income tax on the difference between her "basis" in the property and its sale price. Basis in real property is usually equal to its purchase price. Because it was a lifetime gift, Tina's basis will be the same as Mary's basis of $80,000. Tina will owe taxes on

$200,000 when the property is sold. Even at the lowest capital gains rate of 15%, Tina will owe $30,000 in taxes when the property is sold for $280,000. Both added taxes could have been avoided had a trust been used in planning instead.

**The Lesson**: Assets transferred to a child during the parent's lifetime keep the parent's basis, resulting in income taxes upon the sale of the property. Property that is inherited upon the death of a parent receive a "stepped up" basis of fair market value as of the parent's date of death. If the property is sold immediately upon the parent's death, the child will owe no income taxes on the sale. In this example, this would have saved Tina $30,000 or more.

Whenever property is gifted, no income tax is paid at the time the gift is made. Instead, tax is owed when the property is ultimately sold. The gift recipient's basis in the property is the same as the gift giver's basis. The giver's basis is transferred to the gift recipient.

However, a special exception to this rule exists for inherited property. While the recipient of the gifted property receives a transferred basis from the owner, the recipient of the inherited property receives a new "stepped-up" basis equal to the fair market value of the property on the former owner's date of death. In other words, a parent trying to avoid probate through lifetime gifting in the above example could cost their child a significant amount of avoidable income tax when the property is sold. Accordingly, a parent that wishes to use gifts as a means of avoiding estate planning may cost their children substantial income taxes that could otherwise be avoided through judicious use of trusts or wills.

## The Retention of a Life Estate

Another planning opportunity that uses a lifetime transfer of property is the transfer of a "remainder interest" in real property while retaining a "life estate." This type of lifetime transfer addresses many of the negative consequences listed in the previous section. Using this strategy, the property is split between the "right to use and enjoy the property now," and the "right to own the property later." The former right to exclusive use and enjoyment of the property during the lifetime of the holder is called a "life estate." What is leftover or "remains" following the death of the life tenant is called the "remainder." The owner of real property can give away the future right of ownership of the property, the remainder interest, and yet retain the present exclusive right of use and enjoyment of the property, the life estate. As such, the life estate holder enjoys all the benefits of property ownership during her lifetime, including the exclusive right to use the property free from interference from others, as well as homestead exemption on the property's tax. If the property qualifies for homestead exemption before the transfer of the remainder interest, then the property will continue to qualify for homestead exemption after the transfer of the remainder interest, provided the property is re-registered after the transfer, because the life estate holder has retained a right to exclusive use and enjoyment of the property. During their lifetime, it is, for all practical purposes, as if the holder remains the owner of the property. But, at the life

43

tenant's death, the remainder interest of the property is already owned by the remainder interest recipient, thereby avoiding any need to prove ownership through a probated estate.

The transfer of a remainder interest, with the retention of a life estate, has several advantages over the outright transfer. The most obvious is the fact that the life estate holder has the exclusive use and enjoyment of the property during his lifetime. In other words, if you retain the life estate on land, nobody, including the owner of the remainder interest, can force you to sell the property or evict you from it. You possess the exclusive right to the present interest in the property and can continue to use it as you see fit. Upon the life estate holder's death, however, the remainder beneficiary takes immediate title to the property because that right was already transferred during the lifetime of the life estate holder.

The adverse tax consequences of lost stepped-up basis discussed in the preceding section are wholly avoided through this strategy. The reservation of a life estate is sufficient interest in the property to result in it being counted in the taxable estate of the holder at death, which consequently gives the remainder property owner that stepped-up basis at the life tenant's death that is so valuable.

Although the lifetime transfer of a remainder interest is subject to the gift tax, those gift tax consequences are discounted because the value of what is given away is less than the value of the whole. In other words, if a 65-year-old gives away a remainder interest in a $2 million piece of property, the value of that remainder interest will be based on a percentage of the total value of the whole, or in this circumstance, approximately 32%. Accordingly, the transfer would be treated, for gift tax purposes, as a $640,000 transfer rather than a $2 million transfer. Because the giver has an $11.7 million lifetime gift tax exclusion, the transfer would not require payment of a gift tax, although it would require reporting on a gift tax return.

Of course, the life estate transfer is not without its shortcomings. Most prominent among these is the fact that, as with any lifetime transfer of property, once the remainder interest has been given away, the giver has no right to take it back. In other words, if the giver changes his mind and decides that he wants to give the property to someone else at death, he no longer has the right to make this change. Similarly, if the giver of life estate later needs to sell the property to raise funds for himself, it will, as a practical matter, require the consent of the remainder interest holder(s) too. This is because no rational person would be willing to purchase an interest in the property that only exists for someone else's lifetime. It would be the seller's lifetime, not the purchaser's, which would determine when the life estate ended. As such, the remainder holder effectively has a veto right over any future sale of the property by the life tenant. Additionally, if such a transaction did occur, the life tenant would only be selling the present right to use the property. The remainder tenant would be selling the remainder interest in the property. As such, any sale proceeds would be divided between the life tenant and the remainder owner, with the value of each share being dependent upon the life expectancy of the life tenant owner. At closing, some of the money would be paid to the life tenant, and some of the money would be paid to the remainderman.

As a final matter, federal law permits states to assert a claim against the life estates of Medicaid recipients if the state chooses to do so. While Mississippi has not yet expanded its definition of an "estate" to incorporate life estates, federal law permits it to do so. Accordingly, using this strategy poses a significant risk of losing all or a portion of the property if the life tenant later requires skilled nursing care. Essentially if the life estate holder entered a nursing home and received Medicaid benefits, Medicaid could assert a claim against the beneficiary's estate under federal law. Accordingly, the strategy of attempting to avoid probate by making a lifetime transfer of a remainder interest in retaining a life estate poses a significant risk of loss to all or a portion of that property as the state grapples with ways to cover an ever-expanding Medicaid budget.

## Pay-on-Death Designation

Certain accounts can be transferred upon the death of the owner by naming a beneficiary. Pay-on-death (POD) or transfer-on-death (TOD) designations are permitted on certain types of personal property, like securities, brokerage accounts, bank accounts, and even real estate. By making such a designation, the POD/TOD beneficiary is merely required to show the death of the owner and prove their own identity as the beneficiary. No probate or determination of heirs is required. Additionally, transfers of property in this manner will also give the beneficiary a stepped-up basis in the property, for the same reasons discussed above. As such, this is a very popular alternative to traditional estate planning.

However, transfer of property in this manner is limited to certain types of property. Properties falling outside of these enumerated types cannot be transferred in this way. Until recently, the most notable among these excluded property types was real estate, but in 2020 the law changed to permit pay-on-death deeds. While at first blush, this would appear to be an easy way for individuals to avoid the probate process and avoid wills or trusts. However, in most cases, a probate is still required to convey marketable title to a pay-on-death beneficiary of land because Mississippi law does not protect pay-on-death conveyances from creditor claims. As such, unless one's estate consists only of financial instruments and accounts, he would likely need also to execute a Will or Trust to convey other types of property in a manner different from the default dissent, and distribution statute provides. Another problem with this strategy is the fact that it does not address what happens when a named TOD/POD beneficiary predeceases the owner. When that occurs, the property must pass through the probate estate and, in the absence of a Will, be distributed under the default dissent and distribution statute.

Finally, planning in this manner does nothing to protect the assets from loss to Medicaid in the event of a nursing home stay. The assets remain owned by the original owner until their death, and as such, are subject to creditor claims and remain countable for purposes of qualifying for public benefits.

**Asset Protection Secrets**

# Chapter 5: The Revocable Living Trust

A common and in many ways superior planning alternative to Wills, probate, and lifetime gifts is the creation of a Revocable Trust. With this strategy, a Trust is created during the lifetime of its creator, which holds title to any assets transferred to it. The creator retains the right to make changes to the trust document during his lifetime and usually is named as the manager or "Trustee" of the Trust. Upon the creator's death, the Trust distributes or holds the assets according to the Trust's instructions. Because it is created during the creator's lifetime, it is commonly called a "Living Trust." Since the grantor usually reserves the right to amend or revoke the trust, we call the trust "Revocable." The "Revocable Living Trust" is typically used as an alternative to a Will, with the primary purpose of avoiding the delay and expense associated with probate. It is also an excellent method of ensuring proper lifetime management of an estate by the people selected by the creator on the terms the creator directs without court interference. This chapter will describe how a Revocable Living Trust is formed, how such a Trust operates, and finally, the advantages and disadvantages of Revocable Living Trust-based planning.

## What is a Trust?

A Trust, in its purest form, is just an agreement by one person to manage the property for the benefit of another person. The person that creates the Trust is usually called the "grantor" but may also be known as the "settlor," "trustmaker," or "trustor." Each of these terms refers to the

Trust creator and can be used interchangeably. This is the person that establishes the terms of the Trust and is usually the person that also places property into the Trust. Throughout this Chapter, the term "grantor" will be used to identify the Trust creator, but any of the other terms would also be correct.

The manager of the trust assets is called the "Trustee." The role of a trustee is to manage trust assets for the benefit of the named beneficiary(ies). The trustee must act in the best interest of the beneficiaries, not the trustee's self-interest. We call this person a "fiduciary." The trustee is charged with a duty to act in the utmost care for and on behalf of the beneficiaries of the Trust.

The "beneficiary" of a Trust is the person who receives benefits from Trust assets. If the Trust holds real property, the beneficiary may be entitled to reside in the property or benefit from rents paid on the land. If the Trust holds cash or other liquid assets, the beneficiary may be entitled to the income generated. It may even be entitled to some or all of the principal. Whatever assets that are owned by the Trust are managed and used for the benefit of the beneficiary within the scope of the instructions and limitations contained in the Trust. The Trust itself is simply a set of instructions providing guidance, mandates, and constraints to the Trustee as to what is and is not permissible for the management, sale, and distribution of Trust assets.

Although every Trust has some person or entity filling each of these three rolls of "grantor," "trustee," and "beneficiary," there is no requirement that different individuals fill these roles. It is legally acceptable for the grantor of a Trust, for example, to also be the beneficiary of the Trust. The beneficiary of a Trust can simultaneously be the trustee of a Trust. It is common with most Revocable Living Trusts for the same person to hold all three positions simultaneously.

**Example:** Bob is lying on the beach and decides that he wants to go for a swim. He has a $5 bill in his pocket for a snack and does not wish to get his money wet. He approaches Sally, a sunbather on the beach, and asks her if she will hold his money while he swims and return it when he has finished. Sally agrees, and Bob swims for thirty minutes. Upon his return, Sally gives Bob back his money.

**Result:** This is a straightforward example of a Trust. Bob is the grantor of the Trust. He set the terms of the Trust and funded the Trust with his $5 bill. Sally agreed to be the trustee of the Trust and to manage the $5 during Bob's absence. Her management obligation was simply to protect the asset while Bob swam. Bob was also the beneficiary of the Trust, since Sally, the trustee, was holding the money for Bob's benefit.

Obviously, most Trusts are significantly more complex and formal than the arrangement described in the above example. However, in its simplest form, the above example certainly illustrates the roles and operation of the Trust entity.

**Example:** Bob creates a written Trust agreement. He retains the right, as the Trust creator, to make later changes to the Trust, including the right to amend, restate, or even revoke the Trust. Bob names himself as the trustee of the Trust. The trustee is charged with the management and distribution of Trust assets. The Trust gives complete discretion to the trustee in making investments and distributions from the Trust. Bob's Trust also names Bob as the beneficiary of the trust. As such, the trustee is charged with using the assets owned by Bob's Trust for Bob's sole benefit.

**Result:** Before having a Trust, Bob owned assets in his name, which he managed for himself. After creating the Trust, Bob transferred ownership of his assets out of his name into the name of the Trust. Bob was no longer the "owner" of any assets. Instead, all of his assets were owned by Bob's Trust, which Bob controlled. Bob controls the assets as the creator of the Trust because he retained the right to make changes to the Trust. Additionally, Bob controls the assets as trustee of the Trust. Bob, as trustee, manages the Trust assets for himself as the beneficiary of the Trust.

**Lesson:** Before having a Trust, Bob managed his assets for his benefit. After creating the trust, Bob continues to manage those same assets, but instead of managing them as the owner, Bob manages them as the trustee. Likewise, Bob continues to enjoy and benefit from those same assets, but again, instead of benefiting from them as their owner, he benefits from them as the Trust beneficiary. This Revocable Living Trust has taken assets that were formerly owned by an individual and transferred them into a separate legal entity. Everything else about the assets remains unchanged.

At this point, you may be wondering why anyone would go through the trouble of creating a Trust and transferring ownership of assets when everything continues to be managed by the same people in the same way. The primary reason that people engage in this type of planning is to avoid the expense, delays, and frustrations of the probate process discussed in Chapter Three. As previously discussed, when individuals die, ownership of their land and other assets must usually be settled by a court. The probate process is designed to eventually clear up any ambiguity of ownership after the death of a previous owner. However, most people would prefer to avoid this delay, cost, and frustration. Assets owned by a Trust do not have to go through the probate process because the "owner" of the trust's assets remains the Trust, which has not died. In the example above, if Bob died, his assets would continue to be owned and managed by his Trust. His Trust would, no doubt, name a new trustee to succeed him at his death. Likewise, his Trust would name successor beneficiaries that would benefit from the assets held by the Trust. But since the owner of the assets – the Trust – continues to exist even after Bob's passing, no probate is necessary to determine ownership. They were owned by the Trust while Bob was alive and continue to be owned by the Trust after his death. This is the power of a Revocable Living Trust and the reason that most clients of experienced estate planning firms now incorporate a Revocable Living Trust as part of their modern estate plan.

## Step One-Trust Creation

While there is no requirement that a Trust be in writing to be valid, for purposes of certainty and clarity, Trusts created for estate planning should always be in writing. The writing will describe how the assets of the Trust should be managed, identify the people they are to be managed for, and identify the manager (the trustee). As such, the grantor has a great deal of power and flexibility to determine exactly how his Trust will operate while he is alive, and after his death. Where the grantor also reserves the right to amend, restate, and revoke the trust, the grantor has the ultimate power to make whatever changes she chooses at any time. The retention of this power by the grantor allows the grantor to alter her estate plan at any time before death or incapacity.

While every Trust is drafted to reflect the unique estate planning goals of its grantor, some common themes are used frequently and merit mention. Often, but not always, the grantor of a Revocable Living Trusts retains the right to serve as the trustee of the Trust to manage the assets during their lifetime. Additionally, it is always prudent, although not mandatory, to name an alternate or successor trustee to serve in the event of the grantor's disability, death, or incapacity. Occasionally the initial trustee is someone other than the grantor. This design is used when a grantor wants to turn over management of her day-to-day affairs to a third party immediately, like a bank trust department or accountant, rather than waiting on incapacity.

A Revocable Living Trust should also contain specific instructions regarding the management of the Trust assets during the disability or incapacity of the grantor. This is especially true if the grantor intends to make the assets available for other beneficiaries like a spouse or child.

The Trust should also contain instructions for Trust administration and distribution following the death of the grantor. This may involve an outright distribution of the Trust assets to beneficiaries or may involve retaining the Trust assets for the benefit of the beneficiaries until certain events occur, like finishing college or reaching a certain

age. The Trust could even be designed to retain the assets for multiple future generations, creating a multigenerational trust for the benefit of children, grandchildren, and even great-grandchildren.

## Trustee

The trustee of the Trust is the person designated to manage the Trust assets under the instructions contained in the Trust. The trustee manages the assets for the benefit of the designated beneficiaries. The trustee can be an individual, a group of individuals acting as a committee, or an entity such as a bank or trust company. The trustee is obligated to follow the instructions contained in the Trust agreement and is accountable to the beneficiaries for his actions. Sometimes those instructions are specific, forcing the trustee to take certain actions regularly. "Pay all income annually to the beneficiary," for example. Other times the trustee is given absolute discretion in distributions made from the trust: "The trustee may pay to or on the beneficiary's behalf as much of the principal and income of the Trust as the trustee deems appropriate in the trustee's sole, absolute and unreviewable discretion." The trustee serves as a fiduciary, meaning that the trustee is acting in the beneficiary's best interest, rather than in the trustee's self-interest. The trustee owes a high duty of the utmost care to all the beneficiaries, including future beneficiaries.

While not required, most Trust agreements identify successor trustees who will serve in the absence of the initial trustee. This absence may arise from incapacity, unwillingness to serve, or even the death of the initial trustee. Often the grantor will reserve the right to replace the trustee with anyone of his choosing. The grantor of a

Revocable Living Trust usually appoints himself or herself as the initial sole trustee or jointly with their spouse.

**Beneficiary**

The beneficiary of the Trust is the person for whose benefit the Trust exists. There may be multiple beneficiaries of a trust, such as a husband and a wife, the survivor of them, or even multi-generational beneficiaries, such as spouse, children, and grandchildren.

Frequently, the beneficiary will change depending on the stage of the Trust. For example, a common Revocable Living Trust will name the grantor as the initial beneficiary during her lifetime. Upon the death of the grantor, the Trust will frequently name the grantor's spouse, children, or both as successor beneficiaries to the trust. Sometimes the Trust is designed to provide an outright distribution of assets to the surviving beneficiaries. Other times, the Trust is designed to operate beyond the death of the grantor and manage the Trust assets for the benefit of the successor beneficiaries, but never distribute the assets outright to her. This latter type of Trust is called a Heritage Trust™ and can protect Trust beneficiaries' inheritance from their creditors or divorces. For more information on the benefits of a Heritage Trust™, visit www.familyheritagetrust.com.

**How does the Trust Work?**

Trusts are designed to manage the assets owned by the Trust under the instructions or terms of the Trust. The Trust has no authority over assets that it does not own. Accordingly, individuals wishing to engage in Revocable Living Trust planning to avoid probate must transfer ownership of all assets they want the Trust to control to the Trust. For real estate, this means executing a deed transferring the land to the Trust. For institutional accounts, such as savings and checking accounts or certificates of deposit, this means changing the name on the account or opening a new account in the name of the Trust. To be the most effective, all of an individual's assets should be transferred into the trust. This should be done without fear of losing control because a grantor of a Revocable Living Trust usually reserves the right to amend, restate, and revoke the Trust at any time. Additionally, it is common for the grantor to reserve the right to remove any assets that she chooses from ownership of the Trust.

Whenever a grantor fails to place some assets into the Trust, those assets are not controlled by the Trust. While the grantor will not notice any difference in his ability to manage the assets, successor trustees will have no authority to manage those assets, and terms in the Trust that control distribution of Trust assets will also be of no effect over assets the Trust does not own. This applies both to the authority of a successor trustee to manage assets during the incapacity of a grantor or following the grantor's death. Generally, assets that are held outside the Trust will "pour" into the trust through the use of a "Pour-Over" Will. A "Pour-Over" Will simply provides that any assets owned by a deceased grantor will be poured into the grantor's Trust so that the Trust can control the ultimate distribution of those assets. However, this requires probate, the avoidance of which was probably a significant goal of the grantor in creating the Trust. The delay and expense of the probate process is not avoided for those assets not owned by the

Trust at the grantor's death. Or worse, if the individual fails to fund the Trust and dies without a pour-over will, none of the estate's assets would be managed or distributed by the terms of the Trust, but would instead would revert to the default intestate plan of distribution set out by the State of Mississippi.

Another advantage of Revocable Living Trust planning is control during incapacity. As previously discussed, a well-drafted Revocable Living Trust will contain management instructions that are effective during the lifetime of the grantor during a period of disability. This completely avoids the potential requirement to open a conservatorship for the benefit of an incapacitated individual since the Trust will appoint a new manager without the need for court oversight or direction. The successor trustee is privately appointed to manage the assets under the Trust's instructions.

### The Pour-Over Will

Occasionally, despite the best planning and the best of intentions, a grantor will die without having completed the transfer of their assets into the Revocable Living Trust. As a catch-all mechanism, the grantor should, at the same time he creates a Revocable Living Trust, also sign a Pour-Over Will. As discussed before, a Pour-Over Will refers to a simple will that transfers any assets owned by the decedent at the time of death into the Revocable Living Trust. By executing this type of Will, even assets that are unknown, forgotten, or simply impossible to transfer into the trust during the grantor's lifetime, will nonetheless be controlled by the terms of their trust, albeit after first going through the probate process. While not ideal, this tool at least avoids distribution of assets under different plans like the intestacy laws or an old will that was never revoked, and instead ensures that all assets will pass under the terms laid out in the trust as a unified plan of management and distribution.

Although every grantor should execute a valid Pour-Over Will, it is not recommended that they rely on the Will to fund their Trust since assets that pass through the Pour-Over Will do not enjoy either advantage of creating the Revocable Living Trust – probate and conservatorship avoidance. The Pour-Over Will should instead be viewed as an emergency mechanism that catches any assets that are accidentally missed or impossible to transfer, such as assets received just before the decedent's death.

## Revocable vs. Irrevocable Trusts

While this chapter discusses Revocable Living Trusts, for comparison purposes, some discussion of Irrevocable Trusts should also be helpful to the reader. For the most part, Trusts that are used as Will-substitutes in estate planning are designed to be revocable. However, an alternative to a Revocable Trust is an Irrevocable Trust. As the name implies, the terms of an Irrevocable Trust cannot be easily changed. This is a dramatic distinction from a Trust in which the creator reserves the right to amend, restate, and revoke the Trust instrument. The terms of an Irrevocable Trust generally cannot be revoked or changed in any material manner by the grantor. These types of Trusts are often utilized to achieve more complex planning goals such as taxable estates where significant estate or gift taxes may be owed, or asset protection planning for creditor or

Medicaid protection. While the terms of an Irrevocable Trust cannot be changed at the whim of the grantor, not every Irrevocable Trust is completely inflexible. Depending upon the goal of the Trust, some Irrevocable Trusts can be designed with significant flexibility, including the grantor's ability to make changes to the management and ultimate distribution of assets. Such trusts are "Flexible" Irrevocable Trusts, and the ultimate purpose of the Trust determines the level of flexibility that can be reserved. To learn more about the advantages of Flexible Irrevocable Trusts visit www.FlexibleIrrevocableTrust.com.

**Trust Administration**

Many promoters of Revocable Living Trusts over-emphasize the costs and frustration associated with the probate process and underemphasize the administration and maintenance required of a Revocable Living Trust. While it is undoubtedly true that a properly funded Revocable Living Trust will avoid probate, it is rare that, upon the death of the grantor, some administration of the Trust is not required. Frequently, this administration only involves changing title of the Trust assets from the name of the grantor as the initial trustee of the Trust into the name of the successor trustee. Sometimes this is accomplished with a letter attaching relevant trust pages and a death certificate proving the death of the grantor. Other times it involves filing a new deed or a new certificate of trust.

While not nearly as burdensome or complex as probate, these activities do require some leg work and paperwork and often incur some legal fees. Brokerage companies and banks must be notified of the change in trustee. Tax forms must be completed to assign the Trust a new tax identification number. Creditors must still be located and paid. Much of what is required for the administration of a Trust is the same as needed to administer a probate estate with one notable exception: administration of a Trust requires no court involvement. This single fact is significant because the court-oversight through the probate process accounts for the majority of the expense and delay of probate that frustrates so many. Frequently judges overseeing probate estates will freeze the funds of the estate until the estate is administered to the judge's satisfaction and the court enters its order approving final distribution.

Additionally, any interim activities within a Trust, such as payment of ongoing expenses like electricity and water at a residential property owned by the Trust, or ongoing expenses associated with commercial property, often require separate court authorization for payment in a probate estate. That authorization consists of filing a pleading before the court, incurring legal fees to draft the pleading, and present it to the court to obtain the authorization. In addition to these added expenses, any time that court approval is required, a presentation to the court of the requested relief generally requires a personal appearance before the court, which involves scheduling travel and attendance. The schedules of both the court and the lawyer must be coordinated, which frequently results in delays before the permission can even be obtained.

The administration of a Revocable Living Trust avoids these requirements of obtaining constant court approval and oversight. The grantor is appointing a person that she deems trustworthy enough to make decisions on behalf of the trust beneficiaries, effectively appointing them as a private judge to oversee the administration of their estate. This privatized process saves significant time and money and requires no judge or lawyer. Most trusts can be administered in a matter of weeks. Most probated estates require months or even years to administer. However, contrary to what is suggested by many Revocable Living Trust promoters, the administration process is not free, but in all but the most unusual circumstance the administration cost for a Revocable Trust will be a fraction of the cost of administering a similarly sized probated estate.

## Chapter 6: Powers of Attorney

A power of attorney is a document that assigns the authority held by one person to another person. The person assigning their authority is known as the "principal." The person given the power is called the "agent." Every complete estate plan should also include a durable power of attorney for financial affairs. This document will give a person of your choosing authority over your financial accounts, property interests, and other personal affairs such as lawsuits, insurance settlements, resolution of tax matters, and resolution of employment matters.

Your Durable Power of Attorney for Financial Affairs will typically give one or more individuals authority to act on your behalf, in your absence, in the management of your affairs. In addition to naming a primary agent to manage your affairs, you may also name multiple successor agents, if your primary agent predeceases you, is unavailable, or is simply unwilling to serve. Some generic Powers of Attorney attempt to grant this power over your financial affairs through broad language giving your appointed agent authority to take any action that you could take. However, a better practice is to enumerate the powers that you are granting expressly and, perhaps more importantly, to enumerate any powers that you are not granting expressly. For example, if you wanted your child to have authority to manage your bank accounts for your benefit but did not want to give them the power to sell your house without the consent of others, a carefully drafted Power of Attorney should include the enumerated power over accounts and the specific reservation of authority over real estate.

## Durability

Mississippi law recognizes the authority to create Durable Powers of Attorney. Without this law, your agent would lose the power to act on your behalf upon your incapacity. In other words, if you lost the capacity because of a mental infirmity, then your agent under a power of attorney would likewise lose the ability to act for you. However, with the passage of a Mississippi statute permitting a "durability" provision in all Powers of Attorney, the POA can now survive the incapacity of the principal.

## The Problem with POA's

Despite the existence of this statute, a Power of Attorney does have one significant shortcoming. Although the law gives you the authority to create a Power of Attorney, there is no requirement that anyone actually honor it. Most times, Powers of Attorney are honored, but that is left to the sole discretion of the person with whom the agent is transacting business. Many banks and financial institutions routinely refuse to honor powers of attorney simply as a matter of policy. These institutions are legitimately concerned with the prospect of a fraudulent power being presented only to learn later that the power had been revoked or that the person is acting in their self-interest. Additionally, these institutions are concerned that because of the lack of standardization between the laws of various states, they are unable to efficiently manage the review of powers of attorney under each state's laws.

Accordingly, many institutions are taking the easier and safer path of refusing to recognize any Powers of Attorney.

So, while most people should appoint an agent under a Power of Attorney to exercise authority on their behalf, those same people should likewise recognize that their power may or may not work as intended when the time comes to use it. In such an instance, it will likely become necessary for the appointed agent to seek court intervention to appoint a conservator. The good news is that a chancellor will, in almost all circumstances, appoint the chosen agent as a conservator. The bad news is that the significant cost and delay involved in creating a conservatorship was not avoided.

For this reason, a Revocable Living Trust represents a better and more reliable alternative for lifetime management of assets than the Power of Attorney. For those assets that are owned by a Trust, every institution will be obligated to honor the Trust document, including your designation of trustees or successor trustees. While a change of trustee in a Revocable Living Trust will take some time in the event of your incapacity, it should take significantly less time and be less expensive than the court-ordered conservatorship.

## When does the Power of Attorney take Effect?

A Power of Attorney can become effective immediately upon signing, making the document extremely powerful to the person appointed as agent. The other option is placing a specific condition precedent into the terms of the power of attorney, which makes it ineffective until the occurrence of the condition. A common condition precedent is the disability or incapacity of the principal. In other words, the principal would execute a document which states,

"I give the power to act on my behalf to my agent Joan Smith, but her power does not take effect until I become incapacitated." Such a power of attorney that becomes effective at a future date, or upon the occurrence of a condition precedent, is called a "Springing Power."

Significant consideration should be given before executing a Springing Power. As discussed in the previous section, many institutions are reluctant to honor any Powers of Attorney. If presented with a Power of Attorney that does not even become effective until the principal's incapacity or another future event, any institution would require satisfactory documentation that the incapacity or other condition had been met. In the case of incapacity, proof would no doubt require, at a minimum, affidavits from one or more physicians and possibly other medical records which confirm the disability of the principal to the recipient's satisfaction. Production of these documents may or may not be satisfactory to the institution being asked to rely upon a power of attorney. In any event, it draws into further question the ultimate effectiveness of the document at precisely the time the document is needed most.

In most circumstances, immediate powers of attorney are preferable. If you are reluctant to trust an individual not to act inappropriately at a time that you can actually observe what they are doing (the time before the "Springing Power" becomes effective) is it really prudent to grant such a person authority to act at a time that you are unconscious or otherwise unable to observe their activities? If your distrust of your agent is such that you fear they may act while you are still competent, you should probably re-think whether you have named the best person for the role.  In such circumstances, you may well be better off with a court-supervised conservatorship.

# Chapter 7: Healthcare Documents

## Power of Attorney for Health Care

Just as a principal can give an agent power to act on their behalf for the management of financial affairs, they can likewise give authority to make medical decisions on their behalf. This authority is transferred through a Healthcare Power of Attorney. This document allows you, the principal, to appoint one or more agents to act on your behalf in making health care decisions. While you are competent to make decisions for yourself, the doctors will abide by your wishes. However, in the event of your incapacity, such as an episode of unconsciousness or mental incapacity, a Power of Attorney for Health Care will appoint a clear decision-maker on which the doctors may rely for authority to take a particular course of action.

## Advanced Physician's Directive

A companion document to a Power of Attorney for Health Care is the Advanced Physician's Directive. The Physician's Directive, commonly referred to in many states as a "living will," is a document that expresses your desires concerning specific life-prolonging procedures. The document may state either that you do not wish to be kept alive if you are in a permanent vegetative state or have a terminal condition. Alternatively, the document might state that you want to be kept alive by all heroic measures available for as long as mechanically possible. It is **your** Directive to Physicians concerning **your** life-prolonging procedures.

Consideration should be given as to whether you wish your agent under a power of attorney to have authority to override your wishes expressed your Physician's Directive, or whether you want the Physician's Directive to take precedence.

### HIPAA Release

In the 1990s, the Health Insurance Portability and Accountability Act (HIPAA) was enacted by Congress. Among other things, this act created certain privacy rights for all medical records. Under the terms of HIPAA, a health provider cannot release your health care information unless you have signed a valid release authorizing the disclosure of the records. The release identifies the individuals and the type of medical data that you are authorizing medical providers to release to those individuals. This document becomes vital if your family wants to communicate with your physicians about your condition. Also, where you have appointed an agent under a medical power of attorney, you would not want that agent making decisions for you without the benefit of having first spoken with your health care providers. Accordingly, you must execute a release so that the health care providers can disclose relevant information to your agent so decisions can be made on your behalf.

# Chapter 8: Protecting Your Spouse and Children

## Preserving Your Estate for Those You Love

The primary motivation for most people in planning their estates is the protection of their family. We have already discussed the benefits of planning to ensure that your estate is distributed in the manner that you desire and to the people that you choose. This chapter will discuss some specific strategies that will not only transfer your assets as you wish but will also protect and preserve your legacy for future generations.

One common option in providing for spouses is a simple outright distribution of the entire estate to the spouse. While this is certainly an acceptable option, you should give some consideration to the possibility of your spouse's re-marriage or potential long-term care needs after your death. Additionally, if you have children from a previous marriage, you will likely want to provide for the comfort and well-being of your spouse during his remaining lifetime while also providing some protections for your children upon your spouse's death. You certainly would not want your children accidentally disinherited because you died first, and your spouse remarried. Similarly, you may desire to divide your estate among your children but have concerns that they may squander the estate frivolously or lose it in a divorce. This chapter explores solutions for addressing each of those concerns.

## Providing for the Surviving Spouse

With nearly half of all marriages ending in a divorce, it is not unusual for an estate to involve a second marriage, as well as children on either side from the prior marriage. Similarly, it is not uncommon for a surviving spouse to remarry upon the death of the first spouse. These circumstances require careful planning.

If you have children from a prior marriage, you are likely to be torn between your desire to protect and provide for your surviving spouse's well-being and ensuring your children (not your spouse's children) receive the remainder of your estate. These goals can best be accomplished through the use of a trust created for the benefit of the surviving spouse. We frequently refer to this type of trust as a Heritage Trust™.

A Heritage Trust™ can either be a Testamentary Trust within a Will or a sub-trust contained within a Revocable Living Trust. Such trusts usually provide that the assets placed within the trust are available for the benefit of a surviving spouse. Upon the death of that spouse, the assets are distributed to named beneficiaries. Frequently, the surviving spouse is named as the trustee of that trust. On other occasions, one or more of the children are appointed as trustees or appointed to serve alongside the surviving spouse as co-trustees. Sometimes a surviving spouse is named sole trustee, but if that spouse remarries, their children are then designated as co-trustees. Institutions such as trust companies or banks are also appropriate to appoint as trustees.

The surviving spouse's access to the trust assets can be

unlimited; however, this would usually defeat the overall purpose of the trust, which is to provide for and protect the inheritance of the deceased spouse's children as well as the surviving spouse. Unlimited access would allow the surviving spouse to invade the trust and distribute the assets upon that spouse's death to that spouse's beneficiaries. A more common approach is to give the surviving spouse all of the income from the family trust with limited access to the principal for such things as the surviving spouse's health, or general support needs. This effectively gives the surviving spouse all of the access to funds that he requires but only for legitimate purposes. This would not permit the trust to be raided for inappropriate uses, such as transfers to the surviving spouse's <u>new</u> spouse or transfers to step-children. The Heritage Trust™ can serve to protect your children from your spouse's remarriage while simultaneously providing for the needs of your surviving spouse. Just as importantly, the Heritage Trust™ can also protect your surviving spouse from potential predators – those that might prey on a surviving widow for their own selfish purposes. The assets of the trust would not be available, for example, to your surviving spouse's new spouse, should he choose to remarry after your death. Similarly, if the trust is drafted properly, the trust assets can be made unavailable to your spouse for purposes of public benefit eligibility, such as Medicaid. In that manner, the trust assets would not be required to be spent on long-term care benefits for the surviving spouse but could be available for the spouse's supplemental needs.

Likewise, a properly drafted Heritage Trust™ can

provide protection from a surviving spouse's separate creditors. All of these provisions serve to both provide for the surviving spouse of the marriage yet protect the assets for the children of that marriage or a prior marriage.

### Estate Taxes

Because of increasingly higher exemptions, the threat of estate taxes on an estate is exceedingly rare. However, for estates valued greater than $5 million, some planning for possible estate taxes is still prudent. Currently, there is no Mississippi estate or inheritance tax; however, the federal government has imposed a death tax of approximately 40% of the value of any assets exceeding $11.7 million (in 2021). That tax threshold is scheduled to be reduced to almost half of that effective January 1, 2026, unless Congress takes some intervening action before the sunset of the existing tax law. Accordingly, if you have a large estate and are married, certain additional planning opportunities can effectively double the existing applicable estate tax exemption. This tax minimization is accomplished through the use of the estate tax exemption credit for each spouse. In other words, each spouse is entitled to use their own exemption.

At the death of the first spouse, the estate can split assets between the deceased spouse's and surviving spouse's shares. The maximum value of the then-current exemption amount can be placed within a trust known as a Credit Shelter Trust to fully utilize the applicable exemption credit belonging to the first spouse to die. The remainder of the estate can be paid into a Marital Trust, which would qualify for an unlimited marital deduction.

Thus, regardless of wealth or the size of exemption in effect, there would be no tax incurred at the time of the deceased spouse's death. The assets in both the Credit Shelter Trust and the Marital Trust can be made available to the surviving spouse to provide for their care and support. However, upon the death of the surviving spouse, the assets contained in the Credit Shelter Trust including the growth on those assets, would pass outside the surviving spouse's taxable estate. The assets in the Marital Trust would be included in that spouse's estate but would also be subject to that spouse's separate exemption. Accordingly, for the use of this marital planning, an estate exemption can be doubled and passed to the children or other named beneficiaries free of any estate tax.

An alternative approach would be to file a tax return upon the death of the first spouse and carry or "port" over that spouse's exemption to the survivor. This is referred to as an estate tax credit "portability." While at first glance this approach may seem more straightforward than the creation of separate Credit Shelter and Marital trust shares upon the death of a spouse, reliance on this planning tool alone may eliminate other planning objectives. It could result in higher estate taxes under certain circumstances. Both approaches are appropriate tools to consider, and neither is objectively superior to the other. Planning of this nature is extremely complicated and requires significant forethought, but the potential tax savings in large estates makes the effort worthwhile.

# Protection for Your Children

### Guardianship and Trust for Minor Children

If you have children younger than twenty-one, you should identify the person or persons that you desire to become legally responsible for your children at your death. The legal title for this position is called a guardian. Following the death of both parents, a court will appoint a guardian to be legally responsible for any surviving minor children until they reach the age of majority. In Mississippi, the age of majority is twenty-one. Although a court is not legally bound by your choice or designation of a guardian or co-guardians, a testamentary statement by you declaring your selection for this role would only be ignored or overridden by a court if there was strong evidence suggesting service by the named person was not in the best interest of the minor child.

Such a preference for a guardian is generally declared in your Will. In the absence of such a declaration, the court will be forced to choose among individuals who assert that they should be selected to serve. This frequently involves multiple parties seeking to fill this role. Without the guidance of your preference or intent, the court is forced to exercise its judgment as to who it thinks would best serve the interests of your child, without the benefit of your knowledge, observations, and preferences.

### Distribution of Assets to Minor

If assets are being transferred to the minor child, the court appointing the guardian for the child will also require the funds to be paid into a conservatorship account. Such a conservatorship account will be subject to court oversight, and will often be limited to FDIC insured accounts, which severely limit the potential growth or income from the assets. Additionally, a conservatorship will require annual accountings reported to the court, wherein the court will approve, or in some circumstances disapprove, the chosen uses of conservatorship funds. In many cases, no funds can be spent out of the conservatorship account at all without a separate court order approving each expenditure of those funds. Obtaining such a court order requires filing a petition before the court, and appearing before the court, all of which costs the conservatorship money.

As a more efficient alternative, you can establish a Trust for the benefit of your minor children. Such a Trust would not be subject to direct court oversight and would allow you to determine what types of investments were most appropriate and how the funds could be used for the benefit of your minor children. It would also allow you to name the trustee, who quite frequently is a different person than the individual nominated as guardian for your minor children. Using a Trust to provide for your minor children gives you control over how your assets will be handled for your minor children, as well as who will manage those assets, all without the limitations that a court is likely to impose.

## Chaperone Trust™

Adult children may receive their inheritance outright, immediately at their parent's death, and this is a frequent choice. However, an alternative, which should be strongly considered, is keeping the assets in trust for the benefit of your adult children. There are numerous reasons you should consider this option as an alternative to outright distribution.

If you have a child who has a history of unwise spending habits, such a trust could appoint a third person to oversee the management of the funds to ensure that the assets are not squandered. You have, no doubt, worked hard your entire life to accumulate your estate. Assets distributed directly to your children at your death may be viewed as "found" or "easy" money. Since this is not money that your children earned, they may tend to use the funds liberally or unwisely. You may even have a child with a substance abuse problem, gambling problem, or other compulsions that would result in the rapid loss of your estate. Often for children suffering from such conditions, an outright inheritance is a great hindrance and can even result in severe injury or worse by funding the child's bad habits of choice. In such circumstances, a Chaperone Trust™ could be used to control their access to funds and allow you to appoint a third person to manage those funds and their distribution. You may even choose to add incentive provisions in such a trust, encouraging the child to finish college, obtain a postgraduate degree, or simply hold a job for a stated period. Upon the accomplishment of your stated incentive, additional funds could be released to the child. To learn more visit www.ChaperoneTrust.com.

## Heritage Trust™

You may have children that do not suffer from any compulsive disorders and are prudent with the handling of money. You should nonetheless still consider distributing their share of the estate to them in trust. Such a trust would not be designed to punish them or keep them from receiving their full inheritance. Instead, the trust would be designed to protect their inheritance from third parties, such as creditors from a bad business deal, a tort judgment arising from a car wreck, or perhaps protection from a divorcing spouse. In each of these examples, your children's inheritance could be subject to the claims of third parties without any carelessness or mismanagement by your child but nonetheless resulting in the loss of their inheritance. By leaving their inheritance to them in trust, their inheritance can be protected from such third-party claimants. Yet, the funds can be made liberally available to them for their own needs and enjoyment. Your children can even serve as their own trustee of their Heritage Trust™. To learn more about the Heritage Trust™ visit www.FamilyHeritageTrusts.com.

**Selection of a Trustee**

With every Trust, a trustee must be appointed. In the case of a spousal trust, such as the Marital Trust or the Credit Shelter Trust for the benefit of a surviving spouse, the spouse can be named as the trustee with certain distribution limitations in place, or a third party can be named with complete discretion over distributions. Frequently institutional trustees are selected, such as a bank trust department or separate trust company.

For children's trusts like the Heritage Trust,™ the trustee selection can consist of all the children serving collectively as co-trustees or each child serving as trustee over their own trust share. In the case of a Chaperone Trust,™ you will always want to name a third-party trustee.

This could be another family member, friend, or institutional trustee. In cases where you allow your children to serve as sole trustee of their separate share of their Heritage Trust,™ it would be advisable to consider the appointment a distribution trustee to provide some limitation or expansion to the child's control or right to distribution of assets.

# Chapter 9: Planning for Special Circumstances

Most of the planning opportunities discussed until now involve planning for the "traditional" family – a married couple with independent and responsible children only from that marriage. However, not every family or situation falls within this limited norm. This chapter will address three specific instances of alternate planning considerations for other family circumstances.

## Planning for Special Needs Beneficiaries

The term "special needs beneficiary" generally refers to a beneficiary who suffers from some form of disability. This could be a disability condition arising from birth, such as Down Syndrome or Asperger's, or it may be a condition that occurred later in life such as Alzheimer's, Dementia, or brain injury as a result of an automobile accident. In each of these circumstances, there is a strong likelihood that the special needs beneficiary already qualifies or will in the future need to qualify for public benefits. Many of these benefits are unavailable to people with assets over a few thousand dollars. In other words, many programs that benefit special needs beneficiaries are means-tested and available only to the poor. Frequently, an inheritance of as little as $2,000 by such a special needs child will disqualify them for the government benefits they were previously receiving. A common and unfortunate solution to this problem has been to simply disinherit the child. However, a better solution is to leave that child's inheritance to a Special Needs Trust established for their

81

benefit.

A Special Needs Trust is a trust designed to provide benefits to a special needs beneficiary that will supplement her care but not disrupt, replace or supplant any benefits, public or otherwise, that they were receiving. In other words, if a developmentally disabled child were receiving Supplemental Security Income (SSI) and Medicaid benefits, her assets could not exceed $2,000. If the child receives a $50,000 inheritance, she would immediately lose SSI and Medicaid benefits and would be required to spend the $50,000 inheritance on their own care and support. Once the inheritance was exhausted, the child would again be permitted to reapply for these public benefits. Had the inheritance been left to the child in a Special Needs Trust, the inheritance would not be counted as an available resource to the child and would not cause him to lose the SSI or Medicaid benefits. The $50,000 could be used to enhance their quality of life, such as providing them with stereo equipment, TV, or video games. It could be used to provide health care assistance not otherwise provided by public benefits, such as Lasik surgery or certain non-covered dental procedures. Through the use of a Special Needs Trust, the beneficiary could receive the benefit of their inheritance, which will greatly enhance their remaining quality of life without an adverse impact on government benefits.

Upon the death of the special needs beneficiary, the trust can control where those assets are distributed. Frequently, any assets remaining in Special Needs Trusts are paid to the child's own children or surviving siblings. Other alternatives include leaving the funds to a charity or other family members. Through the use of a Special Needs Trust, you can control the ultimate use and disposition of this portion of your estate. Failure to create a Special Needs Trust may result in loss of valuable public benefits or a requirement that all remaining trust assets be paid to Medicaid upon the child's death.

## Unmarried Couples

Many couples now choose to live together without the formality of marriage. Unmarried Couples must do planning if they desire for their estates to be passed to one another. As previously discussed, if those individuals died without a will, their assets will be distributed under the intestate statute of Mississippi to their descendants or other blood relatives, and not to their significant other. There is no provision for the survivor of a cohabiting couple to receive any portion of their partner's estate. However, through Will-based or Trust-based planning, the significant other can be named as the estate beneficiary. As with married couples, the beneficial interest of the estate may be distributed as an outright distribution or may be retained in trust for the benefit of the surviving partner with any remaining proceeds to be paid to children or other family members.

Often a more important consideration than inheritance planning for these couples is planning for disability. Current health care privacy laws do not provide any allowance for disclosure of medical information to an unmarried co-habituating significant other. If you desire your partner to have access to your health records and to have some role in making health care decisions for you in the event of your incapacity, it is paramount that you execute a HIPAA release giving this individual access to your health care records, as well as a Power of Attorney for Health Care naming this individual as your health care agent. Without these documents, it is unlikely that any health care provider will release any information to this nonfamily member, and the nonfamily member will have no right to make treatment decisions. In fact, in the absence of such documents, family members may be able to bar your significant other from even visiting you.

### Second Marriages and Children of a Prior Marriage

It is a sad reality that nearly half of all marriages end in divorce. Additionally, as a result of improvements in health care, Americans are living longer than ever. As a result of these two factors, it is not uncommon for married couples to be in their second, or even third, marriage. Often there are children from a prior marriage as part of these blended families. Competing planning interests between the desire to provide for one's surviving spouse versus the desire to provide an inheritance to one's own children, must frequently be navigated in modern estate plans. Simply leaving assets outright to the surviving spouse will not ensure an inheritance passes to those children from the prior marriage. Those remaining assets will pass through the estate plan of the surviving spouse, whose own planning likely will likely leave their estate, including any inherited assets, to their own children, leaving the children of the first spouse to die disinherited completely. Even if both spouses execute wills that include one another's children, there is no guarantee that the surviving spouse will not change their plan following the death of their mate.

A more certain alternative would be to leave assets in a trust for the benefit of the surviving spouse, with any remaining assets to pass to the children of the first spouse to die upon the death of the surviving spouse. This will ensure provision for the surviving spouse but protect those assets that remain for the benefit of the children of the first spouse to die. Sometimes this type of planning is further expanded to provide "his", "hers", and "ours" shares of assets during the couple's joint lifetimes, with the separate "his" and "her" assets benefiting both spouses but then passing to their respective children upon the death of the second spouse, and the "ours" share of assets passing equally to all children of both spouses.

# Chapter 10: Planning for Disability and Nursing Home Care

Most of the planning discussed before this chapter focuses on planning for your death. However, some serious consideration should also be made to prepare for asset preservation in the event of a long-term disability. Most people will spend some time in a long-term care facility during their lifetime. If you are over the age of 65, you have a greater than 65% chance of spending some time in a long-term care facility. Modern science has dramatically extended our lifespans. Often, this means that we live well beyond our ability to care for ourselves. This chapter will discuss planning options for paying for long-term care.

## Foundational Documents

As already discussed in previous chapters, everyone should make some plans for the management and control of their assets if they become unable to handle their affairs. At a minimum, this should include the execution of a Durable Power of Attorney and Power of Attorney for Health Care. More comprehensive planning may consist of a Revocable Living Trust, which includes incapacity instructions. Through these documents, your family members or other appointed agents can manage your affairs and act on your behalf if you should become incapacitated. Without these documents, your loved ones will most likely have to obtain a court-ordered conservatorship and manage your affairs under court oversight.

## Options for Care

In the event you become incapable of living independently, you will likely have three options for care. The first, and nearly universally preferred option, is to remain at home with assistance. The assistance may take the form of friends or family members periodically volunteering their services, or it may involve hiring a professional caregiver. Professional non-medical care in the home ranges between $12.00 and $18.00 per hour, depending on the services required and the service provider. These individuals can provide companionship, assist with transportation to physicians, assist with toileting and other personal hygiene needs, and even cooking and cleaning if that is what is required. If your care needs are temporary or are limited to certain activities and times of day, this may be a viable option for your care. However, if your condition requires around-the-clock care, in-home healthcare staffing for a prolonged period is usually prohibitively expensive.

A second option for many people is assisted living. Assisted living facilities generally provide a common dining area and limited services such as housekeeping, meals, and laundry. Some facilities offer more services than others, with some facilities even accommodating Alzheimer's and other memory care patients. The cost of care in these facilities in Mississippi ranges between $3,500 per month to $6,500 per month, depending upon the level of care and assistance required. Residency in these facilities requires some level of independence and generally requires the ability to transfer from a wheelchair to the bed, as they are not skilled nursing facilities.

The care option of last resort is a skilled nursing facility, commonly called a nursing home. Nursing homes provide round-the-clock skilled medical care with on-duty nurses. They assist with feeding, toileting, bathing, and administer medications. Skilled nursing facilities in Mississippi cost between $6,500 per month to $8,000 per month, depending upon the facility and the level of care required.

**How to Pay for Long-Term Care**

There are limited sources of funds available to pay for long-term care. Generally, there are only five sources of funding available. The first source generally looked to is the Medicare program. Medicare provides health care for individuals age 65 and older who have paid more than 40 quarters into the Medicare system. The Medicare system is generally designed to provide care that improves the health of the recipient. Accordingly, it provides only limited payments to nursing care facilities for rehabilitation or convalescence. Medicare will pay 100% of the cost of care for the first 20 days and requires a substantial co-pay for the remaining 80 days of care, which is often covered by supplemental insurance. After 100 days of care in a skilled nursing facility, Medicare will no longer pay for care.

The second source of funding is private funds. Private funds such as savings and retirement funds are always available to pay for assisted care. These funds can be used for any type of care — in-home, assisted living, or nursing home. However, an individual rarely has sufficient income or resources to pay for skilled nursing care for a prolonged period privately.

A third option is long-term care insurance. Long-term care insurance is a benefit available to pay for care at all three levels if the care recipient was fortuitous enough to have purchased it. The funds available for care will vary depending on the terms of the policy. Likewise, the level of care required is also dependent upon the specific terms of the policy. Most policies have a 90 day or longer waiting period before benefits will apply. Additionally, many policies have a lifetime, as well as a daily, cap on benefits. If you have such a policy, you should consult with your insurance advisor to determine whether your existing coverage is sufficient to meet current economic circumstances. If you do not have such a policy, you would be wise to consult with an insurance advisor that specializes in long-term care products. They can advise you as to the availability and cost of various long-term care policies.

The final two options for paying for long term care needs are Medicaid and VA benefits. These options are discussed in Chapters 11 and 12 respectively.

# Chapter 11: Using Medicaid to Pay for Long-Term Care

If the cost of an individual's care needs exceeds their available resources, Medicaid is available to pay for their care as the payer of last resort. Although Medicaid has limited waivers that permit payment for some in-home care and care in certain assisted living facilities, generally, Medicaid is limited to payment for care in a skilled nursing facility. Unlike entitlement programs such as social security and Medicare, which are owed to recipients regardless of income or wealth, Medicaid is a "means-tested" program. If an individual has sufficient means to pay for their own care, they will not qualify for Medicaid benefits. Accordingly, Medicaid qualification is subject to strict asset and income limits. While there are several different Medicaid programs, the one applicable to situations discussed in this chapter are payments made to institutions on behalf of aged, blind, and disabled individuals residing in a skilled nursing facility with limited income. This chapter will discuss the qualification requirements under the Medicaid program for institutional care as well as planning opportunities available to pre-plan for qualification for this benefit without losing all of one's assets.

## Medicaid Qualification

To qualify for Medicaid's institutional care program, an individual must be disabled, reside in a nursing home, and have income and assets below qualifying limits. A Medicaid applicant's monthly income cannot exceed $2,382 (in 2021), and they cannot have countable assets over $4,000.

Even exceeding these limits by one dollar disqualifies the applicant from Medicaid benefits. However, the law allows an applicant with income above $2,382 (in 2021) to still qualify for Medicaid if they execute Qualified Income Trust. Additionally, certain exceptions and exemptions make some assets non-countable toward the $4,000 limit. Both of these are discussed in greater detail below

**Excess Income**

The income limit for Medicaid qualification is $2,382 (in 2021) per month. However, the average cost of a skilled nursing facility in Mississippi is almost $8,000 per month. An individual with no assets and monthly income of only $2,383 would be ineligible to receive Medicaid benefits despite having no assets and insufficient income to pay for the care they needed. They would be almost $5,700 short every month.

Congress addressed such a cruel circumstance by permitting individuals who are disqualified because of excess income to "assign" all of their excess income to a "Qualified Income Trust" for the exclusive purpose of paying for their skilled care or reimbursing the Division of Medicaid for its payment of that care. In other words, an individual with excess income simply needs to sign a document that eliminates all of their income over the income limit for Medicaid qualification purposes. In the example above, the Qualified Income Trust would assign $2.00 per month to the trust, and Medicaid would treat the applicant's monthly income as being below the $2,382 limit. As such, for purposes of Medicaid qualification, the applicant meets the income limit.

**Example:** Bob resides in a nursing home which costs $7,000 per month. Bob's income is $3,500 per month. Bob has no other assets. Bob's income exceeds the income cap of $2,382 per month, and therefore Bob does not qualify for Medicaid.

**Solution:** Bob signs a Qualified Income Trust, which assigns all of his income above $2,382 per month to the trust to be used exclusively for his Medicaid-approved health care expenses or to reimburse Medicaid for its payment of those health care expenses. Bob is now qualified for Medicaid. The Division of Medicaid must treat Bob's income as $2,381 per month.

**Result:** Unfortunately, Bob does not get to keep any of the extra money. All of Bob's money – the income above the $2,382 limit and the income below the limit (except for a $44 per month personal needs allowance) are used to pay for Bob's care in the nursing home. The Division of Medicaid pays any balance. The trust merely creates a legal fiction that treats Bob's income as not exceeding the Medicaid income cap.

The Qualified Income Trust was created by Congress to avoid the cruel and arbitrary result of disqualifying individuals with income that is too low to pay for their own care, but too high to qualify for Medicaid. While the trust is generally known in Mississippi is a Qualified Income Trust, other names for this type of trust are a "Miller Trust" or a 42 USC §1396p (d) (4) (B) trust.

### Exempt Assets
While individuals with countable assets above $4,000 are disqualified for Medicaid benefits, and some assets do not count toward this limit. Such assets are referred to as "non-countable" or "exempt assets." The most common Medicaid exempt assets are:

- A personal residence with equity no greater than $603,000
- An automobile
- Prepaid funerals
- Burial plots for the applicant and their family
- Life insurance with a face value no greater than $10,000
- Designated burial funds not more than $6,000
- Engagement ring
- Retirement accounts if in a monthly payout status

None of the above-described assets are counted for purposes of qualifying for Medicaid benefits. Assets outside of this list are counted, and if the fair market value of those assets exceeds $4,000, then their owner is disqualified from Medicaid until his assets fall below the $4,000 threshold.

**Example 1:** Bob owns a home worth $500,000, a Mercedes-Benz valued at $75,000, a retirement account of $500,000, and a checking account of $3,000. Bob's income is $2,000 per month. Bob has a stroke and enters a nursing home. Does Bob qualify for Medicaid?

**Answer:** Yes. Assuming that Bob instructs his retirement account custodian to make payments from his retirement account in equal monthly payments over his anticipated lifetime, all of Bob's assets other than his checking account are exempt for Medicaid qualification purposes. His income is less than the income cap. His home, car, and retirement account are not counted. His checking account is below the asset limit. Bob qualifies for Medicaid benefits.

**Example 2:** Cindy has an income of $2,000 per month. She does not own a home. She has savings of $10,000 and has no other assets. Does Cindy qualify for Medicaid?

**Answer:** No. Cindy's countable assets exceed $4,000. She is, therefore, disqualified from Medicaid benefits until she spends her savings funds below the $4,000 threshold. The assets of married couples are combined for purposes of this asset limit.

**Example 3:** Randy is married to Jenny. Randy's only asset is a savings account of $3,000. His wife Jenny has a brokerage account valued at $250,000. Randy's income is $3,000 per month, and Jenny's income is $6,000 per month. Randy had a stroke and entered a nursing home. Will Randy qualify for Medicaid?

**Answer:** No. The assets of married couples are combined for purposes of this asset limit. Jenny's brokerage account will disqualify Randy from Medicaid qualification.

## Medicaid Qualification for Married Couples

While the above-described asset and income limitations apply to Medicaid applicants, certain additional safeguards are designed to prevent the impoverishment of a Medicaid applicant's spouse who remains at home. The Medicaid applicant entering or residing in a nursing home is generally referred to as the "Institutionalized" Spouse. A spouse remaining at home is called the "Community" spouse. Married couples' assets are typically treated jointly for purposes of Medicaid qualification. However, certain additional exemptions apply to the assets of a Community Spouse. Specifically, a Community Spouse is entitled to have assets in their name of $130,380 (in 2021). This is commonly known as the "Community Spouse Resource Allowance."

In addition, the Community Spouse's income does not count against the institutionalized spouse. In other words, even though a Community Spouse's income exceeds the income cap of $2,382, their income has no impact on the Institutionalized Spouse's qualification for Medicaid benefits. Spouse's incomes are treated separately for Medicaid qualification purposes. Also, to prevent the complete impoverishment of a Community Spouse, if a Community Spouse's income is less than $3,259.50 (in 2021), the Community Spouse will be entitled to retain enough of the Institutionalized Spouse's monthly income to maintain a household income of $3,259.50 (in 2021) per month.

**Example:** Jack and Jill are married. Each receives a retirement income of $2,000 per month for a total monthly household income of $4,000. Jack must enter a nursing home. Jill will keep her income of $2,000 plus an additional $1,276 from Jack's income to bring her total community household monthly income to $3,216. Jack will retain $44 per month for his personal needs allowance in the nursing home. The balance of his income of $680 will be paid to the nursing home each month, with Medicaid paying all costs over that.

**Example 2:** Jack and Jill own a house worth $500,000. Jack has a $100,000 retirement account. Jill has a $100,000 retirement account. Additionally, Jack and Jill have joint savings of $120,000. Jack has entered a nursing home. If Jack places his retirement account in a payout status with equal monthly payments payable over his anticipated life expectancy and transfers his interest in the savings account to Jill, Jack will qualify for immediate Medicaid benefits. The savings account no longer counts as Jack's asset because it has been transferred to Jill's name and falls within her Community Spouse Resource limit of $128,640. Accordingly, it is not counted toward Jack's qualification limits. Jill's retirement account is exempt since she is a Community Spouse. Therefore, Jack's only asset is his interest in the home, which is exempt.

As will be discussed in more detail in the next section, transfers of assets made within 60 months of applying for Medicaid benefits generally disqualify an applicant from benefits. However, these penalties do not apply to transfers of assets made between spouses.

**Retirement Accounts**

As previously discussed, retirement accounts receive special asset treatment for Medicaid qualification purposes. The retirement account of a Medicaid applicant must be in payout status over their anticipated life expectancy to be treated as exempt. This payout status must be in the form of equal monthly payments over the applicant's life expectancy. Essentially the Division of Medicaid permits retirement account owners to treat their retirement accounts as an income stream similar to as if the applicant had a pension or an annuity. To do otherwise would treat retirees who have Individual Retirement Accounts or 401(k)'s differently than retirees who receive pensions. The pension recipients cannot withdraw a lump sum and instead only receive an income stream over their lifetime. The owner of a 401(k) or IRA, on the other hand, can withdraw funds from that account during retirement, but was planning to withdraw those funds over time during their retirement years. What if the Medicaid applicant's health improves and they return home? A rule requiring them to exhaust their retirement would leave them destitute. At the same time, a similarly situated pension recipient would continue receiving their retirement income just as they had before the illness. To require the IRA or 401(k) owner to liquidate their accounts while permitting the pension beneficiary to continue to receive ongoing lifetime monthly payments, and often a continuation of those payments for a surviving spouse, would cause a severely disparate treatment between those two classes of retirees, both of whom chose to prepare for retirement responsibly, but in different ways. Rather than engage in this disparate treatment and risk the impoverishment of one class, the Division of Medicaid equates both types of retirement income as long as the institutionalized spouse is receiving equal monthly payments from their account. The retirement account of a Community Spouse is exempt, whether it is in payout status or not.

## Transfers of Assets

A reader of the above rules might conclude that a Medicaid applicant could simply wait until the need for skilled care arose and then transfer all of their assets to their children to fall below the Medicaid qualification limits. Such a strategy would work were it not for a provision in Federal law disqualifying any person that transfers assets within 60 months prior to applying for Medicaid benefits. The penalty applies to transfers made by a Medicaid applicant or the applicant's spouse. The disqualification is one month for the average monthly nursing home cost in the state – currently $6,832 (in 2021) – transferred within five years of applying for Medicaid benefits. Each Medicaid applicant must disclose to the Division of Medicaid all "uncompensated transfers" of assets made by them or their spouse over the prior 60 months. The Division of Medicaid then totals all of those transfers and divides them by $6,832 to arrive at the number of months that the applicant will be disqualified from Medicaid. The Medicaid applicant's penalty does not begin until the applicant has both entered the nursing home, applied for Medicaid benefits, and is determined to be otherwise eligible for benefits except for the implementation of the penalty. In other words, to start the penalty clock, the Medicaid applicant must be sick enough to reside in a nursing home, poor enough to meet the means test for Medicaid, and have applied for Medicaid benefits. Only then will the Division of Medicaid calculate the appropriate penalty and determine the applicant's eligibility date.

The purpose of this policy is to prevent precisely the type of last-minute planning that the opening sentence of this section suggests. However, contrary to what some at Medicaid would have you believe, the law does not declare, or even suggest, that the transfer of assets made within five years of a Medicaid application is in any way improper or illegal. The exact opposite is true. Since the law specifically provides a consequence for just such transfer, it anticipates and even makes allowance for the conduct. The law does not prohibit or prevent transfers made within five years of application, but instead acknowledges the appropriateness of such transfers and gives a consequence for that permitted act. In other words, as long as an individual is willing to be disqualified for benefits for a period of time, it is perfectly permissible, and often even advisable, to make transfers of assets within the five-year lookback.

**Example:** Bill has $68,000 and earns $4,000 a month in retirement. Bill enters a nursing home costing $7,000 per month. Bill gives $68,000 to his son and applies for Medicaid benefits. Medicaid applies a ten-month disqualification penalty as a result of Bill's transfer and determines that he would be eligible for benefits beginning the 11th month. For the next ten months, Bill pays $4,000 per month to the nursing home. Bill's son pays an additional $3,000 per month from the funds that his father gifted him, for a monthly total of $7,000. At the end of the 10th month, Bill's penalty has expired, and he is qualified for Medicaid. Bill's son still has $36,000 from the funds that his father gave him.

The law neither prohibits nor discourages the transfer of assets by a Medicaid applicant. It merely imposes a consequence that Medicaid applicants and their families should calculate to determine the most desirable result. The frequent claims of many, including government caseworkers, that, "Transfers made for purposes of qualifying for Medicaid are illegal," or "Gifts made by a Medicaid applicant must be immediately returned," are simply incorrect statements of the law. Congress provides a mathematical calculation to determine a period of ineligibility and expects people to make rational decisions based upon that calculation. There is nothing immoral or illegal about doing math or applying the law in a manner most beneficial to a Medicaid applicant or their family. To the contrary, the opposite is true.

**Planning for Immediate Medicaid Eligibility**

This chapter has summarized the basic rules that apply to Medicaid applications. For Medicaid applicants that already fall within the statutory asset limits, there is often little if anything necessary to do in advance of applying for Medicaid. But for families of applicants that have responsibly prepared for retirement, been frugal and saved during their lifetimes, and have accumulated assets above these qualification limits, the above rules can have a devastating effect. Applied in their purest form, a couple that has managed to build a nest egg of $500,000 for their retirement years can be faced with the devastating possibility that they must spend $371,360 on nursing home care before either of them qualifies for Medicaid. What's worse, all of those years of preparation and saving will leave an at-home spouse with resources of only $128,640. Compare that outcome to a similar couple that was less frugal, enjoying new cars, frequent vacations, and other luxuries throughout their lives, but managing only to have savings of $100,000. An ill spouse from the second couple would immediately qualify for Medicaid benefits, leaving that Community Spouse with essentially the same resource cushion as the more frugal and responsible couple. In essence, the Medicaid eligibility system rewards people that act irresponsibly and punishes more fiscally responsible families by taking or requiring them to spend their assets. With such outcomes, it is easy to understand why most people find the current system unfair.

Fortunately, there are additional strategies that permit families to save significantly more of their assets than the Community Spouse Resource Allowance provided by law. While the details of such strategies are highly technical and well beyond the scope of this book, the reader should be aware that such strategies generally allow for half to two-thirds of a Medicaid applicants' assets to be fully protected immediately before entering a nursing home, without any preplanning. Occasionally circumstances even allow 100% of the applicants' assets to be protected. The notion that an individual has "waited too late" and now has no options available for safeguarding anything is simply false. There are always strategies that can protect significantly more than a basic application of the rules provide. Because of the highly technical nature of Medicaid law, applying such strategies is never a do-it-yourself endeavor. Before engaging in immediate Medicaid eligibility planning, an applicant's family should seek the counsel of a Certified Elder Law Attorney specializing in crisis Medicaid asset protection techniques. If a lawyer tells you that nothing can be done, or you've waited too late, **then see another lawyer**. There are **always** strategies that can save significantly more assets than the basic rules provide.


## Planning in Advance of Incapacity

While it is good to know that half or more of a Medicaid applicants' assets can be protected using techniques provided by law in a crisis, such an outcome still results in a substantial loss of the family's assets. Rather than take that risk, many families wisely choose to plan in advance of their need for skilled care to maximize the protection over all of their assets. Such planning is prudent and available. While every circumstance is different, one commonly used strategy for Medicaid asset protection is the Legacy Trust™. A Legacy Trust™ is a flexible irrevocable trust that is designed to maximize a grantor's control over assets held by the Trust, maximize the tax advantages available to the grantor and his family, and yet simultaneously make the assets unavailable to Medicaid. In essence, individuals that implement this strategy create a legal entity over which they retain significant control, including the right to control investments, control distributions, and even change Trust beneficiaries, yet make the assets a completely unavailable for Medicaid purposes.

While transfers of assets to these Trusts will result in an eligibility penalty if a Medicaid application is filed within five years of a transfer, once 60 months have passed, the assets are completely unavailable to Medicaid. In essence, individuals that want to protect their assets from Medicaid can create a Trust that they can control but which holds assets fully protected from and unavailable to Medicaid. The assets in the Legacy Trust™ will still benefit from the step-up in basis when the grantor's children ultimately inherit the assets. The assets in the Legacy Trust™ will be protected from the potential creditors or divorce of the grantor's children. And the grantors can continue to exercise substantial control over the trust assets, including investment decisions, residing in residential property owned by the trust, and even making periodic changes to the ultimate beneficiaries of the trust assets at the grantor's death. As with any Trust, the specific terms and clauses are highly technical, and if drafted incorrectly, the Trust will lose its tax and Medicaid advantages. Accordingly, anyone doing planning of this nature should always consult with an appropriate expert like a Certified Elder Law Attorney or an Estate Planning Law Specialist. Planning of this nature should never be attempted as a do-it-yourself project. The stakes are too high, and the impact of a minor mistake will be devastating.

## Chapter 12: Veterans' Benefits

The Veterans Administration provides a unique benefit to disabled wartime veterans. The Veteran's Pension Benefit is a supplemental income program available to wartime veterans and their surviving spouses that meet certain health, service, income, and net worth requirements. This program is vastly underutilized due largely to a lack of knowledge by many who qualify. An additional impediment to qualification is the complex set of rules that govern eligibility, delays, and hurdles in the application process, and a reluctance or inability of many VA employees to be candid and forthcoming with information about the program. This Chapter provides a summary of the eligibility requirements for this program and offers some planning suggestions for qualification.

### 1. Service Requirements

The veteran must have served at least: one day during World War II, the Korean Conflict, the Vietnam Conflict, or served one year during the Gulf War. Additionally, the veteran must have been on active duty at least 90 consecutive days. There is no requirement for the veteran to have served in an actual combat zone or to have a disability associated with their service.

### 2. Medical Needs

The veteran must be permanently and totally disabled to receive a pension. The VA will provide additional income known as "Regular Pension," "Housebound Pension," or

"Aid and Attendance" if the veteran or the veteran's surviving spouse cannot leave their home without assistance, is blind, a patient in a nursing home because of mental or physical incapacity, or proves a need for aid and attendance based upon the performance of activities of daily living such as bathing, feeding, dressing, or toileting. There is no requirement that the veteran's incapacity be service-related.

### 3. Income Limitations

The applicant's income reduces the veteran's pension benefit. If household income exceeds the available monthly pension, they are not eligible for any benefits, notwithstanding their incapacity or qualifying wartime service. However, "income" for purposes of qualifying for this benefit is a net calculation after reduction for qualifying medical expenses. Accordingly, an individual veteran with an income of $3,000 per month, but an assisted living facility's expense of $2,500 per month, would have a net income for VA purposes of only $500 per month, rather than their gross $3,000 income.

### 4. Asset Test

A VA Pension applicant cannot have countable assets over $130,773 (in 2021). If the veteran is married, both spouse's assets are counted toward this limit. However, several assets are non-countable. These exempt assets include the veteran's home, household furnishings, and vehicles.

### Applying for Benefits

The Veteran's Pension Benefit can only be applied for by the applicant veteran, an individual acting on a one-time basis on behalf of the veteran, a veteran's service organization, or an accredited veteran's agent. Because of the complexity of the application process, many applicants find it beneficial to seek the assistance of a professional when applying for these benefits. However, only accredited claims agents and representatives can apply on a veterans' behalf. Unfortunately, many unscrupulous individuals seek to scam or prey upon veterans. Check the credentials of anyone seeking to assist with your VA application at https://www.va.gov/ogc/apps/accreditation/index.asp to ensure they are qualified and authorized by the VA to assist.

**"Wartime" Defined**

For a wartime veteran to qualify for the special pension benefit, the veteran must have served 90 days of active duty, and at least one day of service must be during a "time of war." For veterans of Desert Storm, the service requirement has been expanded to 1 year of active duty. The benefit requires "time" of war, not "place" of war. Accordingly, many veterans and their widowed spouses are surprised to learn that they qualify for this benefit even though the veteran has never seen active combat. The Veteran's Administration defines "periods of war" as:

- **World War I**: April 16, 1917, through November 11, 1918

- **World War II**: December 7, 1941, through December 31, 1946

- **Korea conflict**: June 25, 1950, through January 31, 1955

- **Vietnam conflict**: August 5, 1964, through May 7, 1975

- **Gulf War**: August 2, 1990 and continuing

## Medical Needs

The special pension provides compensation to wartime veterans or their surviving spouses who require the regular attendance of another to assist with activities of daily living, such as eating, dressing, bathing, toileting, and other forms of personal care. This compensation is to assist them with paying for those attendant services. Individuals who are blind or reside in a nursing home because of mental or physical incapacity also qualify for this benefit. Likewise, much of the care provided in assisted living facilities qualifies as aid and attendance.

## Asset Limits

Not every disabled wartime veteran or widowed spouse of a wartime veteran qualifies for this benefit. In addition to service and disability requirements, the Veteran's Administration also has qualifying financial limits. Some assets are exempt, and therefore not counted, such as homes and vehicles. However, any assets that are not exempt and are owned by or available to the veteran or their spouse are counted toward the veteran's $130,773 (in 2021) asset limit. The Veteran's Administration counts cash, stocks, certificates of deposit, annuities, along with other forms of liquid assets. Additionally, retirement accounts, Revocable Living Trusts, and most Irrevocable Trusts are also counted toward a veteran's asset limits.

**What If a Veteran has Too Many Assets**

For veterans or their widowed spouse that otherwise qualify for this benefit except for the fact that they exceed the asset limitation, certain planning techniques are permitted to meet the financial qualifications. Many of these strategies involve converting countable resources into non-countable resources, such as purchasing a more expensive home, purchasing household items like as appliances and electronics, purchasing a prepaid funeral, purchasing an exempt automobile, making improvements to an existing home, paying off a mortgage, and repaying unsecured debt

**What About Transfer of Assets**

Prior to 2018, the Veterans Administration did not prohibit or penalize transfers of assets. Accordingly, a veteran with excess resources could simply give any excess assets away to family or place them into a non-countable trust, and qualify for benefits immediately. Unfortunately, that changed on October 18, 2018, when the VA put in place a prohibition against transferring covered assets within three years of an application of VA Pension benefits. Now any transfer of covered assets within 36 months of an application for VA Pension benefits will result in disqualification of benefits for one month for every $2,295 transferred.

**Example:** Wartime Veteran has non-exempt assets of $153,723 and otherwise qualifies for Aid & Attendance benefits. One hundred thirty thousand seven hundred seventy three dollars is exempt, but because he is over the asset limit by $22,950, he transfers that sum to his son and applies for A&A. He will be ineligible for VA A&A benefits for ten months. In month 11, following the transfer, he will qualify for the benefit. The transferred amount, $22,950, divided by the transfer penalty divisor of $2,295, results in a 10-month disqualification penalty.

### The Patriot Trust™

Because of the 3-year lookback and disqualification penalty, veterans that would otherwise qualify for this benefit through their service record but would be disqualified because of their net worth would be prudent to transfer any disqualifying assets well in advance of their need for care. By doing so more than 36 months before needing the benefit they can pre-qualify themselves for the maximum benefit amount well in advance of their need for assistance and qualify immediately when their need for assistance arises.

While the prudence of making such a transfer is clear, the harder question is "where" to transfer the assets. Transfers to a spouse will not help because the married couple's assets are counted jointly. Asset transfers to children may sound logical until you consider the risks inherent in such a strategy. A gift of assets to a child is exactly that – a gift. The child can do with their newly received money whatever they choose – purchase a new house, buy a fancy car, take lavish vacations. The only restrictions on the child's expenditures are their self-discipline. Even if the recipient child did not see the new-found money as an early inheritance, they may nonetheless "borrow" some of the funds for a purchase or investment, fully intending to repay them later when their financial situation has improved. Even in the absence of such behavior, assets given to a child are subject to that child's creditors – creditors that you may not know about; creditors that arise after your gift; creditors that result from lawsuits; creditors that arise from a bad economy. What used to be "your" money becomes "your child's" money, without any protection from these threats.

Additionally, the gifted money, or a significant portion of it, could be lost in your child's divorce or custody battle, falling under the Chancery Court's jurisdiction in the resolution of your child's domestic disputes. Chances are that any transfers of funds would not be intended to be an early inheritance, but rather intended to merely be held by the child for your benefit later if you needed them, but that would not be how the law treated such a transfer. They would be treated as gifts.

A far better solution is to create a separate entity – a trust – designed to hold the funds and protect them from a spendthrift child, a child's divorce, and all of your child's current and future creditors. The Patriot Trust™ is an

111

irrevocable trust designed specifically for those purposes The trust is designed to retain all of the positive tax treatments such as tax-free treatment of gain on sale of your residence, homestead property tax exemption, and the stepped-up basis upon your death, while eliminating the threats of your child's creditors, divorce, or spending sprees. The funds would no longer be treated as yours for VA purposes, but simultaneously would not be treated as your child's either, until your death. Veterans whose net worth exceeds the asset limitations would be wise to consider the creation of a Patriot's Trust™, along with the transfer of any excess resources into that trust. Thirty-six months after the transfer of assets into the trust, the veteran or their widowed spouse would be fully qualified to receive VA pension benefits while simultaneously retaining the maximum amount of control over their assets that the law permits, and further while protecting them from a child's imprudent behavior. As an added bonus, assets transferred into the Patriot's Trust™ also start the five-year protection clock for Medicaid qualification purposes for those same assets.

The rules governing trusts are complex, requiring a thorough understanding of common-law, statutory law, tax law, Medicaid statutes and regulations, and Veteran Administration statutes and regulations. Accordingly, veterans considering such a strategy should seek the advice of a Certified Elder Law Attorney that actively practices in this area.

## How Much Will the VA Pay

There are three different pension benefits under this VA program – Regular, Housebound, and Aid & Attendance. The Special Pension benefit pays the following monthly and annual amounts to the respective classifications of disabled veterans:

| Monthly/Annual | Regular | Housebound | A&A |
|---|---|---|---|
| Veteran | $1,161 / $13,931 | $1,419 / $17,024 | $1,936 / $23,238 |
| Veteran w/ Spouse | $1,520 / $18,243 | $1,778 / $21,337 | $2,296/ $27,549 |
| Widowed Spouse | $778 / $9,344 | $952 / $11,420 | $1,245 / $14,934 |

Unfortunately, the maximum benefit amount is not automatically paid to all qualifying veterans. Instead, the benefit amount sets an income floor for veterans. Benefits are reduced by income. In other words, if a veteran's income is more than the benefit amount they are entitled to receive, they receive no benefit under the program. At first glance, this would seem to disqualify all but the very poorest of disabled veterans. However, the income is first reduced by the veteran's medical expenses. In other words, the income used for qualification calculation is not gross income, but net income after reduction for medical expenses.

**Example:** Wartime Veteran has an income of $3,000 per month and resides in an assisted living facility at a cost of $4,000 per month, and has assets below the asset limit. Wartime Veteran meets all the criteria for Aid & Attendance benefits with a spouse. While $3,000 per month in income exceeds the A&A monthly benefit amount of

$2,295, Wartime Veteran's monthly income for VA purposes is actually a loss, -$1,000, because the monthly cost of assisted living reduces his income for VA purposes. Wartime Veteran qualifies for the full $2,295 per month.

### Interaction between VA Benefits and Medicaid

Frequently the care needs of individuals progress as they age. They may start by needing assistance a few hours per day to remain comfortable at home. The Aid & Attendance benefit is perfect for this situation as it will provide compensation for sitters needed those few hours each day. However, as the veteran's needs increase, they may then move into a nursing home. While VA Aid & Attendance benefit will assist with payments for nursing home care, it is unlikely to cover the entire bill. The cost of such skilled care usually far exceeds most individual's income in retirement, even with the added benefit of A&A. Once in a nursing home, most people require Medicaid benefits to pay for their care. If that individual has moved assets into a Patriot Trust™ or used other techniques to shelter excess resources to qualify for the VA benefits, they could be ineligible for Medicaid benefits because of the transfer penalty incurred by moving assets into the trust.

While transfers of assets are ignored after 36 months for purposes of VA benefits, those same transfers will continue to disqualify from eligibility for Medicaid benefits for an additional 24 months because of Medicaid's longer 60-month lookback. Therefore, extreme care should be taken anytime that planning strategies are used to qualify for VA benefits. There is always the possibility that those care needs may increase, and Medicaid benefits will be needed later. Accordingly, every plan to receive VA benefits must also always incorporate an alternative plan for qualifying for Medicaid benefits. This planning should most frequently be accomplished using the services of an Accredited VA Agent that is also a Certified Elder Law Attorney so that every facet can be addressed in the planning. With the help of such professionals, many veterans and their widows can receive monthly pensions that make a dramatic difference in needed care that they otherwise could not afford. This benefit is frequently the difference between an individual languishing at home trying to make do with what they have because of insufficient resources, versus spending their final years in the comfort and safety of an assisted living facility or at home with all the daily help that they need.

## Chapter 13: Where do I go from Here?

It is never too early to begin estate planning. A well thought out estate plan can be one of the best gifts you could ever give to your loved ones. Done properly, the estate planning process is not painful. On the contrary, once you have completed your estate plan, you will no doubt have the peace of mind that comes from knowing that you have secured your assets and planned your affairs to benefit yourself and your loved ones.

### Find an Attorney

Although there are several options available for "do-it-yourself" estate planning, the advice and consultation of an attorney should always be sought if you desire to provide any protection for your heirs. Any estate plan other than an outright distribution of assets to named beneficiaries will benefit from the advice and counsel of a qualified estate planning attorney.

There are several different ways you can find a competent Estate Planning Attorney:

- Ask your friends, neighbors, and relatives if they know of a good Estate Planning Attorney. If they had a good experience with a particular lawyer, it is likely, you will also have a pleasant experience.
- Search the membership rolls of respected estate planning organizations that are more than mere membership organizations. Some organizations, like the National Academy of Elder Law Attorneys, are mere membership organizations.

Any lawyer willing to pay a $450 annual fee can join and get listed. While membership in such an organization might indicate something more than a mere passing interest in an area of law, it does nothing to confirm the aptitude or qualifications of its members. As such, in the author's opinion, such organizations do little to inform the quality of member lawyers. Other organizations, however, are limited to strict ethical and academic criteria. The National Elder Law Foundation, for example, is the only organization recognized by the American Bar Association with the ability to certify Elder Law attorneys as specialists in the field.

- Similarly, the National Association of Estate Planners and Counsels is the only organization recognized by the American Bar Association with the ability to credential lawyers as Estate Planning Law Specialists. Holders of these designations must pass rigorous academic testing, continuing education, and peer review. Resources such as these are far more helpful in finding experts in the fields of Estate Planning and Elder Law than mere membership clubs.

- Another criterion to consider is the teaching experience of the lawyer. A lawyer with an active law practice that also teaches as faculty at a law school is generally recognized as an expert's expert – the top of their field.

## Meet with the Attorney

Once you have identified prospective attorneys, you should schedule an initial interview. Some attorneys offer a free consultation. Those in high demand will generally charge a fee for the first meeting, much like you would expect a surgeon or other specialist to charge for their time.

The initial meeting is an excellent opportunity for you to get to know the lawyer and to find out whether you are comfortable working with her, are satisfied with their knowledge of the law and ability to communicate, and whether you share the same values. It also allows the lawyer to get to know you and to assess whether the representation would be a good fit, or whether you could better be served by someone else.

After an initial consultation with you, the attorney should be able to make recommendations for your planning needs and provide you with a quote for the cost of the attorney's services. You should never hire an attorney without first having a thorough understanding of the scope of work to be performed and precisely how you will be charged.

## Preparing for Your Meeting

Once you have located an estate planning attorney, you should consider many of the issues already addressed in this book so that you can provide the attorney with your planning goals. Some of the problems you should be prepared to address include:

- Who do you want to serve as your executor or trustee?
- Who do you want to handle your financial

affairs during your lifetime if you are unable to manage your affairs?

- Who do you want to make medical decisions for you if you are unable to make them yourself?
- Are you concerned about avoiding probate?
- Are you willing to put some or all of your assets into a trust during your lifetime to avoid probate?
- Are you concerned about the possibility of requiring nursing home care during your lifetime?
- Have you made adequate plans to pay for skilled care?
- Are there any concerns that you want to make sure your estate plan covers?

## Storing Your Estate Planning Documents

Once you have executed your estate planning documents, you should store them in a secure location. Many people keep their Will and other essential documents in a bank safe deposit box or home safe. Others simply keep their records at home in a location readily accessible to them. In any event, it is crucial that you keep copies of your estate planning documents in a separate location. You should consider scanning your estate planning documents into a PDF format and storing them electronically off-site if your lawyer does not already provide you with electronic copies. In any event, your Executor needs to know the location of your planning documents and have access to them. This means that if your documents are stored at a bank safe deposit box, your Executor should be named on the account to have access to the box without having to obtain a separate court order to retrieve your Will and other estate planning documents.

**Periodically Review Your Plan**

One of the biggest mistakes people make is the failure to review their plan periodically. Things change as the years pass. Safeguards that you put in place for the protection of a child may no longer be necessary. Your asset values today may be considerably higher or lower than when you drafted your plan several years ago. The state and federal tax laws periodically change. The plan drafted to maximize the benefits under an old estate tax law may have no current advantage. Instead, the new law may have adverse income tax consequences that your plan should now address. You should meet with your attorney every three to five years to review your estate plan. In this way, you can ensure that your estate plan is up-to-date and covers your current goals as they change from time to time. Additionally, you should review your estate plan if any of the following occur: the death of an heir; a significant change in the value of your estate; change of mind as to your plan of distribution of assets; change of mind as to who you want to serve as your Executor or your agents; changes in the law that may affect you; marriage; divorce; life-threatening illness; or change of state of residence.

**Conclusion**

Congratulations! Having completed this book, you are

now, no doubt, better informed about the options available to you in planning your affairs and how those options may benefit you and your family. By purchasing and reading this book, you have taken the first steps toward protecting your assets and your loved ones from unnecessary threats to your estate. Whether your planning goals are simply to make lifetime transfers of assets to loved ones, or to engage in comprehensive tax and asset protection planning, the options and solutions offered in this book have hopefully enlightened you as to many planning opportunities available, and why certain planning options may be more beneficial to your circumstance. Your next step should likely be to seek out a qualified estate planning attorney. Once you have created a plan, you will have the peace of mind of knowing that you've done those things necessary to protect yourself, your loved ones, and the results of your life's work.

# Do You Have Questions?

MORTON LAW FIRM, PLLC

is pleased to offer
readers of this book a

# Complementary 15 Minute Consultation

If you have completed this book and have questions you wish to discuss, the author is pleased to extend to you the opportunity of a free 15-minute phone consultation. To take advantage of this special offer, simply call the number below and schedule your call.

## (601) 925-9797

*Thank you for reading.*
*We hope this book has been helpful to you or someone you love.*

Made in the USA
Middletown, DE
23 July 2022